AFRICA: PROGRESS AND PROBLEMS

ETHNIC GROUPS IN AFRICA

AFRICA: PROGRESS AND PROBLEMS

ETHNIC GROUPS IN AFRICA

Elizabeth Obadina

Frontispiece: A member of the Bayei people of Botswana poles his dugout canoe, or *mokoro*, along the shallows of the Chobe River.

Mason Crest
450 Parkway Drive, Suite D
Broomall, PA 19008
www.masoncrest.com

Printed and bound in the United States of America.

CPSIA Compliance Information: Batch #APP2013. For further information, contact Mason Crest at 1-866-MCP-Book

First printing
1 3 5 7 9 8 6 4 2

Library of Congress Cataloging-in-Publication Data

Obadina, Elizabeth.
Ethnic groups in Africa / Elizabeth Obadina.
p. cm. — (Africa: progress and problems)
Includes bibliographical references and index.
ISBN 978-1-4222-2939-2 (hc)
ISBN 978-1-4222-8884-9 (ebook)
1. Africa—Ethnic relations—Juvenile literature. 2. Ethnic conflict—Africa—Juvenile literature. 3. Ethnicity—Africa—Juvenile literature. 4. Africa—Social conditions—Juvenile literature. I. Title. II. Series: Africa, progress & problems.
DT15.O23 2013
305.80096—dc23
2013013027

Africa: Progress and Problems series ISBN: 978-1-4222-2934-7

Table of Contents

AFRICA: PROGRESS AND PROBLEMS

AIDS and Health Issues

Civil Wars in Africa

Ecological Issues

Education in Africa

Ethnic Groups in Africa

Governance and Leadership in Africa

Helping Africa Help Itself: A Global Effort

Human Rights in Africa

Islam in Africa

The Making of Modern Africa

Population and Overcrowding

Poverty and Economic Issues

Religions of Africa

THE PROMISE OF TODAY'S AFRICA

by Robert I. Rotberg

Today's Africa is a mosaic of effective democracy and desperate despotism, immense wealth and abysmal poverty, conscious modernity and mired traditionalism, bitter conflict and vast arenas of peace, and enormous promise and abiding failure. Generalizations are more difficult to apply to Africa or Africans than elsewhere. The continent, especially the sub-Saharan two-thirds of its immense landmass, presents enormous physical, political, and human variety. From snow-capped peaks to intricate patches of remaining jungle, from desolate deserts to the greatest rivers, and from the highest coastal sand dunes anywhere to teeming urban conglomerations, Africa must be appreciated from myriad perspectives. Likewise, its peoples come in every shape and size, govern themselves in several complicated manners, worship a host of indigenous and imported gods, and speak thousands of original and five or six derivative common languages. To know Africa is to know nuance and complexity.

There are 54 nation-states that belong to the African Union, 49 of which are situated within the sub-Saharan mainland or on its offshore islands. No other continent has so many countries, political divisions, or members of the General Assembly of the United Nations. No other continent encompasses so many distinctively different peoples or spans such geographical disparity. On no other continent have so many innocent civilians lost their lives in intractable civil wars—15 million since 1991 in such places as Algeria, Angola, the Congo, Côte d'Ivoire, Liberia, Sierra Leone, and Sudan. No other continent has so many disparate natural resources (from cadmium, cobalt, and copper to petroleum and zinc) and so little to show for their frenzied exploitation. No other continent has proportionally so many people subsisting (or trying to) on less than $2 a day. But then no other continent has been so beset by HIV/AIDS (30 percent of all adults in southern Africa), by tuberculosis, by malaria (prevalent almost everywhere), and by less well-known scourges such as schistosomiasis (liver fluke), several kinds of filariasis, river blindness, trachoma, and trypanosomiasis (sleeping sickness).

Africa is among the most Christian continents, but it also is home to more Muslims than the Middle East. Apostolic and Pentecostal churches are immensely powerful. So are Sufi brotherhoods. Yet traditional African religions are still influential. So is a belief in spirits and witches (even among Christians and Muslims), in faith healing and in alternative medicine. Polygamy remains popular. So does the practice of female circumcision and other long-standing cultural preferences. Africa cannot be well understood without appreciating how village life still permeates the great cities and how urban pursuits engulf villages. Africa can no longer be considered predominantly rural, agricultural, or wild; more than half of its peoples live in towns and cities.

Political leaders must cater to both worlds, old and new. They and their followers must join the globalized, Internet-

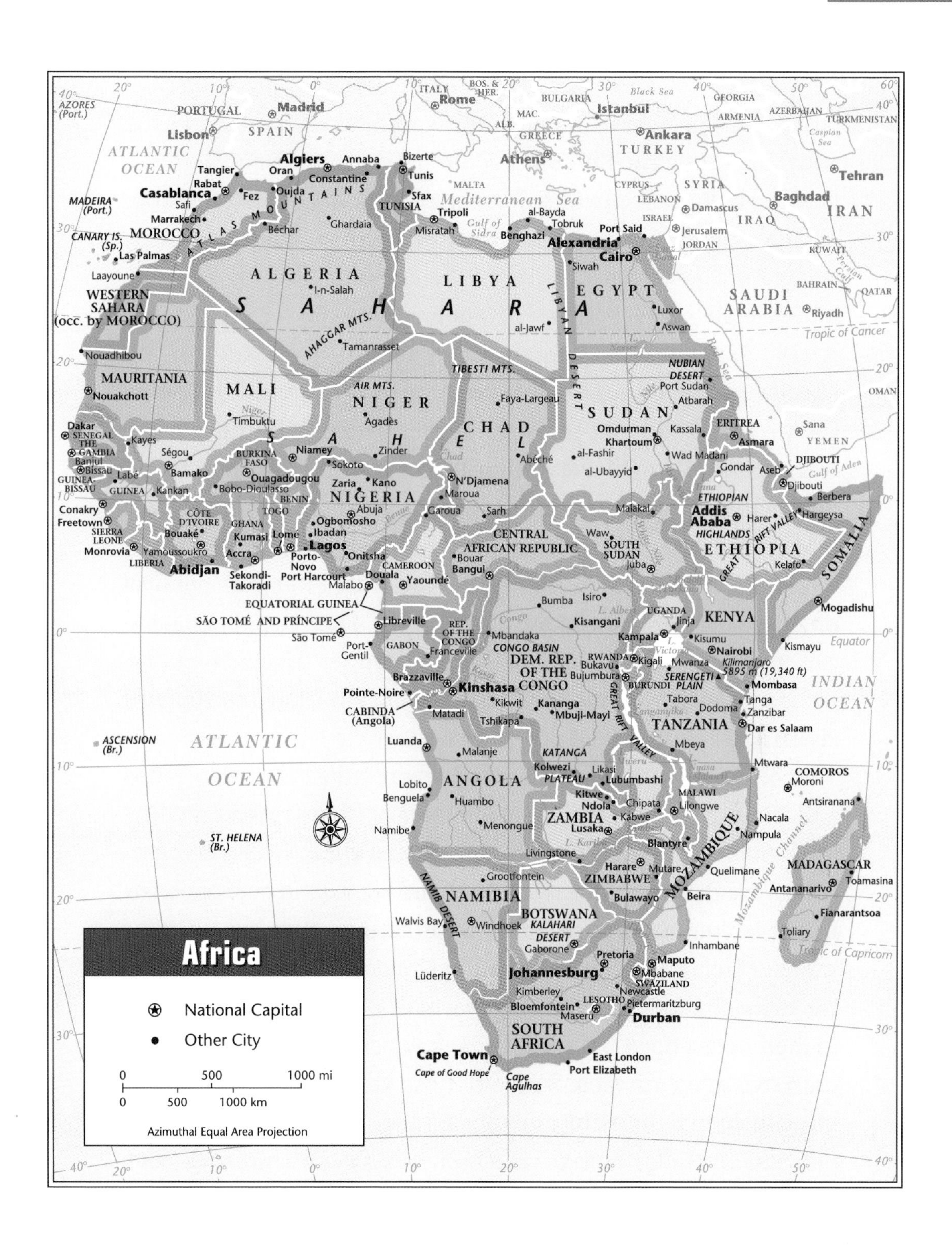
Africa
National Capital
Other City
0 500 1000 mi
0 500 1000 km
Azimuthal Equal Area Projection
AZORES (Port.)
PORTUGAL
Madrid
SPAIN
Lisbon
ATLANTIC OCEAN
MADEIRA (Port.)
CANARY IS. (Sp.)
Las Palmas
Tangier
Rabat
Casablanca
Safi
Marrakech
Fez
Oujda
Oran
Algiers
Annaba
Constantine
Bizerte
Tunis
Sfax
TUNISIA
ATLAS MOUNTAINS
MOROCCO
Béchar
Ghardaia
Tripoli
Misratah
Laayoune
WESTERN SAHARA (occ. by MOROCCO)
ALGERIA
I-n-Salah
AHAGGAR MTS.
Tamanrasset
SAHARA
LIBYA
LIBYAN DESERT
al-Jawf
ITALY
Rome
BOS. & HER.
MAC.
ALB.
BULGARIA
GREECE
Athens
Istanbul
Ankara
TURKEY
Black Sea
GEORGIA
ARMENIA
AZERBAIJAN
TURKMENISTAN
Caspian Sea
Tehran
IRAN
Baghdad
IRAQ
SYRIA
Damascus
CYPRUS
LEBANON
ISRAEL
Jerusalem
JORDAN
KUWAIT
Persian Gulf
BAHRAIN
QATAR
SAUDI ARABIA
Riyadh
MALTA
Mediterranean Sea
Gulf of Sidra
al-Bayda
Benghazi
Tobruk
Port Said
Alexandria
Cairo
Suez Canal
Siwah
EGYPT
Luxor
Aswan
Tropic of Cancer
Red Sea
NUBIAN DESERT
Port Sudan
Atbarah
OMAN
Nouadhibou
MAURITANIA
Nouakchott
MALI
Timbuktu
Niger
AIR MTS.
NIGER
Agadès
TIBESTI MTS.
Faya-Largeau
CHAD
SAHEL
Zinder
Niamey
Sokoto
Abéché
SUDAN
Omdurman
Khartoum
Kassala
al-Fashir
Wad Madani
al-Ubayyid
ERITREA
Asmara
Sana
YEMEN
DJIBOUTI
Djibouti
Aseb
Gulf of Aden
Gondar
Dakar
SENEGAL
THE GAMBIA
Banjul
Bissau
GUINEA-BISSAU
Kayes
Ségou
Bamako
Labé
GUINEA
Kankan
BURKINA FASO
Ouagadougou
Bobo-Dioulasso
Zaria
Kano
NIGERIA
N'Djamena
Maroua
Lake Chad
BENIN
TOGO
Abuja
Ogbomosho
Ibadan
Lagos
Onitsha
Conakry
Freetown
SIERRA LEONE
CÔTE D'IVOIRE
GHANA
Bouaké
Kumasi
Lomé
Monrovia
Yamoussoukro
LIBERIA
Abidjan
Accra
Sekondi-Takoradi
Porto-Novo
Port Harcourt
Malabo
Douala
Yaoundé
CAMEROON
Benue
Garoua
Sarh
Malakal
ETHIOPIAN HIGHLANDS
Addis Ababa
Harer
Hargeysa
Berbera
SOMALIA
GREAT RIFT VALLEY
ETHIOPIA
Kelafo
CENTRAL AFRICAN REPUBLIC
Bouar
Bangui
Waw
SOUTH SUDAN
Juba
White Nile
Nile
EQUATORIAL GUINEA
SÃO TOMÉ AND PRÍNCIPE
São Tomé
Libreville
GABON
Port-Gentil
REP. OF THE CONGO
Franceville
Mbandaka
Congo
CONGO BASIN
Bumba
Isiro
Kisangani
L. Albert
UGANDA
Jinja
Kampala
KENYA
Kisumu
Nairobi
L. Victoria
Mogadishu
Kismayu
Equator
Kilimanjaro 5895 m (19,340 ft)
SERENGETI PLAIN
Mombasa
RWANDA
Kigali
Bukavu
Mwanza
Bujumbura
BURUNDI
DEM. REP. OF THE CONGO
Kasai
Brazzaville
Kinshasa
Pointe-Noire
CABINDA (Angola)
Matadi
Kikwit
Kananga
Mbuji-Mayi
Tshikapa
Tabora
Dodoma
Tanga
Zanzibar
Dar es Salaam
TANZANIA
INDIAN OCEAN
Lake Tanganyika
Mbeya
ASCENSION (Br.)
ATLANTIC OCEAN
Luanda
Malanje
KATANGA PLATEAU
Kolwezi
Likasi
Lubumbashi
Mtwara
COMOROS
Moroni
Lobito
Benguela
ANGOLA
Huambo
Kitwe
Ndola
Chipata
MALAWI
Lilongwe
Lake Nyasa
Antsiranana
Nacala
Nampula
Mozambique Channel
Namibe
Menongue
ZAMBIA
Kabwe
Lusaka
L. Kariba
Zambezi
Blantyre
MOZAMBIQUE
ST. HELENA (Br.)
Livingstone
Harare
Mutare
Quelimane
ZIMBABWE
Beira
MADAGASCAR
Antananarivo
Toamasina
Grootfontein
NAMIB DESERT
NAMIBIA
Bulawayo
Fianarantsoa
Walvis Bay
Windhoek
BOTSWANA
KALAHARI DESERT
Gaborone
Inhambane
Toliary
Tropic of Capricorn
Lüderitz
Pretoria
Johannesburg
Maputo
Mbabane
SWAZILAND
Newcastle
Kimberley
LESOTHO
Bloemfontein
Maseru
Pietermaritzburg
Durban
Orange
SOUTH AFRICA
Cape Town
Cape of Good Hope
Cape Agulhas
East London
Port Elizabeth

penetrated world even as they remain rooted appropriately in past modes of behavior, obedient to dictates of family, lineage, tribe, and ethnicity. This duality often results in democracy or at least partially participatory democracy. Equally often it develops into autocracy. Botswana and Mauritius have enduring democratic governments. In Benin, Ghana, Kenya, Lesotho, Malawi, Mali, Mozambique, Namibia, Nigeria, Senegal, South Africa, Tanzania, and Zambia fully democratic pursuits are relatively recent and not yet sustainably implanted. Algeria, Cameroon, Chad, the Central African Republic, Egypt, the Sudan, and Tunisia are authoritarian entities run by strongmen. Zimbabweans and Equatorial Guineans suffer from even more venal rule. Swazis and Moroccans are subject to the real whims of monarchs. Within even this vast sweep of political practice there are still more distinctions. The partial democracies represent a spectrum. So does the manner in which authority is wielded by kings, by generals, and by long-entrenched civilian autocrats.

The democratic countries are by and large better developed and more rapidly growing economically than those ruled by strongmen. In Africa there is an association between the pursuit of good governance and beneficial economic performance. Likewise, the natural resource wealth curse that has afflicted mineral-rich countries such as the Congo and Nigeria has had the opposite effect in well-governed places like Botswana. Nation-states open to global trade have done better than those with closed economies. So have those countries with prudent managements, sensible fiscal arrangements, and modest deficits. Overall, however, the bulk of African countries have suffered in terms of reduced economic growth from the sheer fact of being tropical, beset by disease in an enervating climate where there is an average of one trained physician to every 13,000 persons. Many lose growth prospects, too, because of the absence of navigable rivers, the paucity of ocean and river ports, barely maintained roads, and few and narrow railroads. Moreover, 15 of Africa's countries are landlocked, without comfortable access to relatively inexpensive waterborne transport. Hence, imports and exports for much of Africa are more expensive than elsewhere as they move over formidable distances. Africa is the most underdeveloped continent because of geographical and health constraints that have not yet been overcome, because of ill-considered policies, because of the sheer number of separate nation-states (a colonial legacy), and because of poor governance.

Africa's promise is immense, and far more exciting than its achievements have been since a wave of nationalism and independence in the 1960s liberated nearly every section of the continent. Thus, the next several decades of the 21st century are ones of promise for Africa. The challenges are clear: to alleviate grinding poverty and deliver greater real economic goods to larger proportions of people in each country, and across all countries; to deliver more of the benefits of good governance to more of Africa's peoples; to end the destructive killing fields that run rampant across so much of Africa; to improve educational training and health services; and to roll back the scourges of HIV/AIDS, tuberculosis, and malaria. Every challenge represents an opportunity with concerted and bountiful Western assistance to transform the lives of Africa's vulnerable and resourceful future generations.

OVERVIEW: A CONTINENT OF VAST ETHNIC DIVERSITY

Africa is a region of enormous human diversity. Genetically, there is more variability among Africa's people than among people anywhere in the world. Africa also contains vast ethnic diversity: by some estimates, the continent's 54 countries are home to as many as 3,000 distinct ethnic groups.

An ethnic group may be defined as a large group of people with a common ancestry, a shared historical and cultural tradition (including a common language), and an identifiable historical territory. Until relatively recently, Westerners used the word *tribes* to refer to the indigenous peoples of Africa. But in some circles that is now considered an offensive label, as it is said to carry connotations of primitiveness. However, the term still appears widely in literature and is still freely used within Africa, by Africans.

Samburu men, Kenya. The ancestors of the semi-nomadic Samburu, who are related to the better-known Maasai people of Kenya and Tanzania, are believed to have migrated from the Sudan.

ETHNICITY AND HISTORY

Ethnic identity has played an important role in human history, serving as a major factor in the

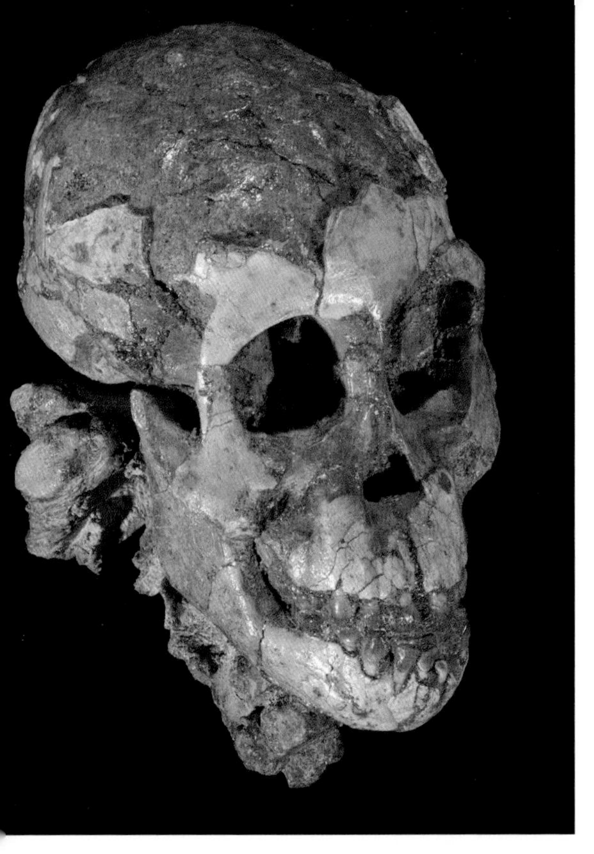

This fossil skull of an *Australopithecus afarensis* child, dated to 3.3 million years ago, was found in the Afar region of Ethiopia in 1999. Paleontologists believe *A. afarensis* is an ancestor of the *Homo* genus, which includes modern humans. The fossil evidence indicates that humans first evolved in East Africa, around present-day Kenya and Ethiopia, then spread to the rest of the continent and the world.

organization of certain societies, in motivating large-scale migrations, and in shaping interactions among different peoples. Historically, many conflicts have pitted one ethnic group against another.

Nevertheless, the importance of ethnicity should not be overstated. Even when ethnicity is undeniably a factor in some historical event, other forces are virtually always at work as well. States—whether ethnically homogeneous or not—act to secure vital economic resources, which often brings them into competition or conflict with other states. Individual leaders frequently make momentous decisions out of personal motivations such as a desire for power, wealth, or acclaim. Religion may be a more powerful unifying force than ethnicity. History provides numerous examples to illustrate these points.

"TRIBAL" EXPLANATIONS OF AFRICAN HISTORY

The 19th century was a period of intense scientific interest in the origins and development of the human race. Among the scientific disciplines that emerged during the 1800s was anthropology, the study of the physical and cultural development of human populations across time and place. The 19th century was also a period when European nations colonized the African continent, about which—especially the interior regions of sub-Saharan Africa—

A rock painting made by the San people, who were the original inhabitants of southern Africa. Some 15,000 such paintings have been discovered. The most ancient are more than 27,000 years old.

the outside world had previously known very little. Western anthropologists followed early explorers and colonial administrators into Africa. In most areas, the social scientists found few if any written records and little archaeological evidence to help them make sense of how African cultures had developed. Absent knowledge of an African history—of, for example, the rise and fall of African states or the contributions of important individuals—African politics, social relations, and cultural development came to be understood almost exclusively within a "tribal" context. Africa's story was reduced to a simple narrative of tribes with different racial characteristics, ritual practices, customs, and even "typical" behaviors.

Such an approach to understanding the arc of Western civilization would, needless to say, have been unthinkable. But this one-dimensional view of Africa—a view implying that Africans were simple, indeed primitive—fit the colonialist agenda, which was focused above all on exploiting the continent's resources.

Today there is a much greater understanding of African history, and in academic circles the colonial-era view of a primitive Africa whose development could be adequately explained through ethnic or tribal factors is thoroughly discredited. But for many parts of the continent there are still large gaps in the historical record. Scholars have been working to patch together a more complete picture of African peoples' pasts using evidence from disciplines such as archaeology, genetic analysis, comparative cultural studies, and linguistics. Much of the evidence is subject to differing interpretations.

HIGH STAKES

The scientific inquiry is not simply a matter of academic interest. Ethnic groups—or, frequently, leaders promoting an ethnic agenda—often base their claims on a particular interpretation of history that may or may not be valid. The assertion that, for example, the ancestors of a certain group occupied a particular territory first may be used to assert that group's right to land or resources. The claim that two ethnic groups are historically related, whether scientific evidence bears that out or not, may be used to justify greater influence than either group by itself would wield. Or, conversely, a supposed link between two groups may be exploited to stir up grievances among, and thereby unify, members of a third group. In this environment, seemingly innocuous activities—such as the collection of data for census returns or the making of purely academic linguistic recordings—become highly contentious exercises. Scientists and statisticians find themselves on the front lines of ethnically colored disputes.

Such disputes often explode into deadly violence. The reasons for this are highly complex and vary from country to country, but analysts from various points on the ideological spectrum tend to focus on a different set of factors.

Conservative commentators frequently explain Africa's ethnic conflicts in terms of long-standing hatreds caused by "natural" ethnic differences, like language, lifestyles, and religious schisms. The idea that contemporary ethnic conflicts might have ancient roots is explored in Chapter 3 of this book, which analyzes ethnicity in sub-Saharan Africa's oldest nation, the Sudan.

Left-wing analysts tend to blame ethnic conflict in Africa on the corrosive legacies of colonialism and even the slave trade. The consequences of colonial policies that favored the creation of efficient administrations over nation building are considered in Chapters 3, 4, and 5, on the Sudan, Nigeria, and Rwanda, respectively.

Many analysts in the center of the political spectrum believe that Africa's continuing ethnic problems largely reflect the failure of African countries to develop stable democratic institutions. Such institutions, these observers argue, would provide a means of resolving ethnic disputes without bloodshed. This theme will be explored within the context of Nigeria. Chapter 4 examines the ethnic balancing act pursued by Nigeria, where politics is dominated by three main ethnic groups and policies that support quotas and the idea of "ethnic entitlement."

Another theme this book explores is the view, advanced by some economists and other social scientists, that what are commonly held to be ethnic conflicts are in many cases not ethnically based—at least not under the traditional definition of an ethnic group as a group whose members share a common ancestry,

Some observers cite fundamental ethnic or "tribal" differences as a cause of many African conflicts. Other experts believe the focus on ethnicity conceals the real issue: division of scarce resources in an impoverished continent.

language, culture set, and ancestral territory. Ethnicity, according to this view, often becomes an issue only after a conflict has already developed, and communal grievances are then attributed to it. Moreover, many observers point out that ethnicity is an elastic concept: ethnic groups are social constructs susceptible to change rather than objective, historically based realities. Groups referred to as ethnic groups may be unified not by their shared ancestry, culture, and so on, but merely by the shared interests and common actions of their members.

In Africa, where poverty is widespread, competition over scarce resources has often triggered ethnic conflict. Sometimes ethnic tensions have been stoked by unscrupulous leaders seeking to secure their power. Even crime lords have manipulated ethnic rivalries to ensure access to illicit riches.

The subject of ethnic groups in Africa is far too wide-ranging and too complex to treat comprehensively in a book of this length. This volume instead attempts first to provide an overview of Africa's ethnic diversity, organized around linguistic evidence (Chapter 2). The rest of the book then offers detailed case studies, from three countries in sub-Saharan Africa, illustrating the many difficulties Africans face in attempting to construct peaceful, harmonious societies.

2 LANGUAGE AND ETHNICITY

In 2013, according to the United Nations Population Division, there were more than 1 billion people living in Africa, with over 750 million living in the part of the continent that lies south of the Sahara Desert. The diversity of Africa's people is evidenced by the large number of languages spoken on the continent—2,058, according to one recent estimate (dialects, or regional variations, bring the total to 3,000 or more). With only about 14 percent of the world's population, Africa is home to some 30 percent of the world's languages, according to linguists.

Language is arguably the most important marker of ethnicity. Fundamental to a person's self-identity, it is the glue that binds ethnic groups together, social scientists say.

In Africa, where written records and durable archaeological remains are scant, the study of African languages provides valuable evidence of where ethnic groups originated, when they migrated, and where they went. In a continent

(Opposite) Four major language families on the African continent—Afro-Asiatic, Nilo-Saharan, Niger-Kordofanian, and Khoisan—comprise more than 2,000 distinct tongues. This map shows the distribution of the language families, including some of the most widely spoken languages.

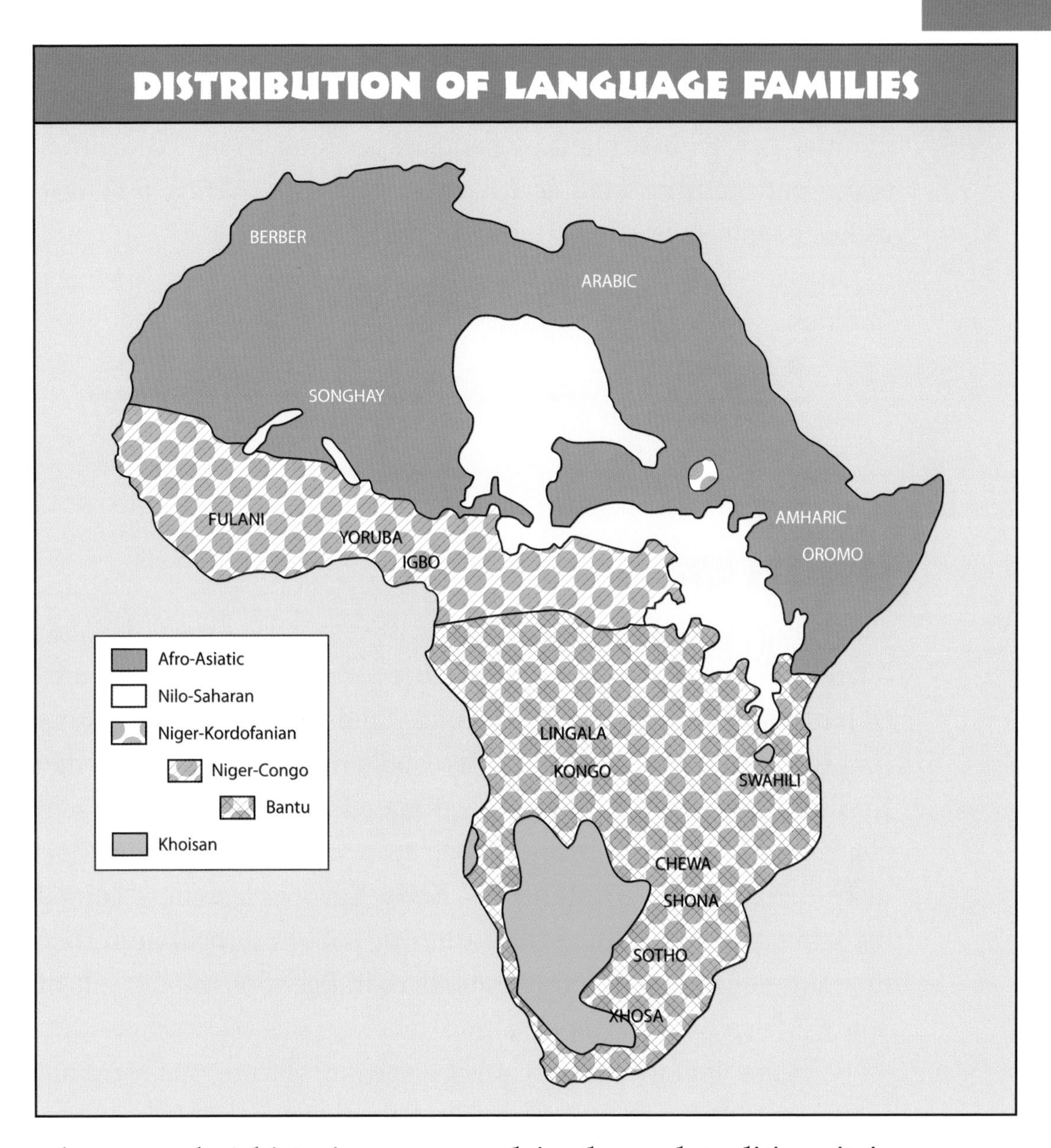

where peoples' histories are rooted in the oral tradition, it is especially appropriate that language is a major descriptor of identity.

Linguists and anthropologists seeking to trace the history of Africa's peoples may focus on groups' mother tongues, but in modern Africa most individuals are multilingual and can read, write, or speak an overarching language such as English, French, Arabic, or Swahili in addition to their first language. Most people are also able to understand the basics of several other local languages in spoken form, so even this fundamental index of ethnic identity can be overrated by scholars seeking to explain differences and conflict among Africa's people. In Africa language unites people as much as it divides them.

African languages are classified into four major language families:

- Khoisan
- Nilo-Saharan
- Afro-Asiatic
- Niger-Kordofanian.

KHOISAN

The Khoikhoi and San people of southwest Africa speak ancient "click" languages called Khoisan. There are fewer than 30 recorded languages in the Khoisan language family. The largest is Nama (or Khoekhoegowab), which is spoken in Namibia. Today Khoisan speakers total only an estimated 300,000–400,000 people. Khoisan speakers include people once called "Bushmen" or, more derogatively, "Hottentots." Early European settlers coined the latter name to imitate the stuttering speech impediment they thought they heard afflicting the talk of indigenous inhabitants of South Africa's Cape region.

Scholars believe that Khoisan speakers were the original inhabitants of much of Africa. They lived throughout the continent's central, eastern, and southern areas until pushed to the inhospitable Kalahari Desert fringes of Namibia and Botswana by Bantu-speaking African peoples migrating southward over the past thousand years, and Europeans colonizing northward from the Cape over the last 400 years. Many of South Africa's Bantu people have incorporated some of the Khoisan "clicks" into their own languages, making them regionally distinct from the rest of Africa's Bantu speakers.

A San woman and child, Namibia. Bantu migrations forced the San onto inhospitable land around the Kalahari Desert.

Maasai dancers, Kenya. Today an estimated 350,000 Maasai, who traditionally pursued a nomadic or semi-nomadic way of life as herders of livestock, live in Kenya.

NILO-SAHARAN

Almost 50 million people living in the savanna lands bordering the deserts of western and northeastern Africa speak a Nilo-Saharan tongue. There are nearly 200 languages in the Nilo-Saharan language family, which some scholars believe is linked with the extinct Meroitic language spoken by the ancient Kushites of Nubia.

It is a matter of intense academic debate as to whether Nilo-Saharan speakers migrated southward along the Nile from the direction of Egypt, or northward from a possible prehistoric homeland in the Nuba Mountains of central Sudan. Whichever the case, over the past 2,000 years Nilo-Saharan speakers spread westward along the southern fringes of the Sahara Desert until they reached the Niger River in present-day Mali. There they built a series of ancient kingdoms, including the fabulously wealthy Mali and its successor, medieval Songhay. Other kingdoms followed, such as the thousand-year-old Bornu emirate in Kanuri-speaking northeastern Nigeria, and the Darfur Sultanate, located along the present-day border between Sudan and Chad.

Other groups of Nilo-Saharan speakers who probably left the Sudanese/Ethiopian highlands more than 2,000 years ago began drifting southward, along the Nile. They were the ancestors of the Alur people living in present-day Uganda and the

Originally from the Arabian Peninsula, Bedouin have been roaming the desert lands of Egypt and North Africa with their herds of camels, goats, and sheep since the seventh century A.D. Increasingly, however, they have come under pressure to adopt a settled way of life.

Democratic Republic of the Congo; the Datooga in Tanzania; and the Luo, Maasai, and Turkana peoples of Kenya.

AFRO-ASIATIC

The third great family of African languages is Afro-Asiatic, a group of 372 languages spoken across North Africa, across the northern areas of most West African states, and throughout the Horn of Africa. Its speakers total more than 350 million people. Afro-Asiatic branches into two main divisions: a major division that includes the Egyptian, Berber, Chadic, Omotic, and Semitic language subfamilies; and a minor division called Cushitic. The Chadic subfamily includes one of sub-Saharan Africa's most widely spoken tongues, Hausa.

The Semitic subfamily of mainstream Afro-Asiatic languages is particularly important to Africa as it includes Arabic, along with Hebrew. A Semitic subgroup of languages includes Ethiopia's Amharic and Tigrinya, as well as Tigre, which is spoken in neighboring Eritrea.

Within the minor Cushitic division of Afro-Asiatic languages a smaller, separate Cushitic subfamily branch includes Somali, Oromo, and Afar and is said by some scholars to be derived from the language spoken by the ancient Egyptians. Their equally ancient neighbors, the Beja people, migrated to the Red Sea hills in eastern Sudan more than 5,000 years ago and still speak their own Cushitic language, Bedawiye.

NIGER-KORDOFANIAN

The languages spoken mainly in the Kordofan provinces of south-central Sudan form one isolated branch of the Niger-Kordofanian language tree. The other branch, or phylum, is called Niger-Congo. It includes nearly 1,500 languages spoken by more than 500 million Africans. Niger-Congo is the biggest language phylum in the world and contains the majority of African

Fulani women and children, Kano, Nigeria. The traditionally pastoralist Fulani are spread across several West African countries.

languages spoken today.

Most Africans living south of the Sahara speak a language deriving from the Niger-Congo subfamily of Niger-Kordofanian. Within the Niger-Congo subfamily are six major groups (most of which are found within West Africa):

- West Atlantic (including Fulfulde, spoken by 9 million Fulani pastoralists across northern Nigeria, Chad, and Cameroon and in parts of Senegal).
- Mande (including Dyula, Manding, Mende, and Soninke, spoken by descendants of the founders of the ancient Islamic empires of Ghana and Mali).

- Voltaic (including Dogon, spoken by a Malian people who claim descent from ancient Egyptians).

- Adamawa-Eastern (also known as Adamawa-Ubangi languages, which are spoken in eastern Nigeria, Cameroon, Chad, southern Sudan, and the Central African Republic).

- Kwa (which includes the major southern Nigerian languages of Yoruba, Igbo, and Bini, also called Edo; Ewe, spoken in Togo and Ghana; and Fon, spoken by the descendants of the old Dahomey slaving kingdom in the present-day Republic of Benin). The Twi subgroup of Kwa includes the Asante language, spoken in Ghana.

- Benue-Congo (of which the Bantu subgroup is the biggest and best known).

BANTU

Approximately 275 million people—about a third of all sub-Saharan Africa's inhabitants—speak a modern Bantu language. They are thought to be descended from ancient inhabitants of Nigeria and Cameroon.

Scholars believe that about 2,000 years ago, Bantu speakers began leaving their homelands in the hills between the Benue and Cross Rivers in present-day southeastern Nigeria and western Cameroon. Some of these migrants made their way southward until they reached the mighty Congo River of central Africa. Others followed a second route and walked east, through the grasslands bordering the central forests of Africa and into the Great Lakes area. From there they moved into eastern and southern Africa. These Bantu speakers were the ancestors of—among many other ethnic groups—the Herero, Luvenda, Ndebele, Northern Sotho, Ovambo, Sesotho, Setswana, Shona,

Swazi, Xhosa, and Zulu peoples of southern Africa. They were also the ancestors of the Kikuyu, Ganda, Nyoro, Rundi/Rwanda, and Swahili speakers of eastern Africa, as well as Lingala speakers in countries along the Congo River of central Africa. In Nigeria's eastern borderlands and in western Cameroon, small pockets of people still speak Bantu languages like their east, central, and South African distant cousins.

SUDAN: ANCIENT LAND, ONGOING CONFLICTS

Since the mid-1950s, the region known as Sudan has been convulsed by almost continuous strife. For most of its history the country of Sudan, which became independent in 1956, was torn by a civil war between northern and southern factions. Ultimately, the southern part of Sudan became independent in July 2011 as a consequence of the long conflict. The civil war, as well as recent violence in Sudan's western Darfur province, have generally been depicted as ethnically based conflicts. However, the reality—particularly in the case of the Darfur conflict, which some observers have labeled the "first genocide of the 21st century"—may not be quite so clear-cut.

Sudan and South Sudan straddle the middle reaches of the Nile River and its tributaries. From prehistoric times, diverse groups have passed through this region, which formed part of a corridor out of, and back into, Africa. Over the course of millennia, Sudan became a melting pot for African and Middle Eastern cultures.

ETHNIC GROUPS IN SUDAN
EGYPT
Lake Nasser
Red Sea
LIBYA
CHAD
ERITREA
ETHIOPIA
CENTRAL AFRICAN REPUBLIC
DEMOCRATIC REPUBLIC OF THE CONGO
UGANDA
KENYA
NILE NUBIAN
BEJA
Port Sudan
Nile River
Atbara River
Omdurman
Khartoum North
Khartoum
Kassala
Wad Medani
Gedaref
White Nile
Blue Nile
El Obeid
Meidab
Zaghawa
Masalit
Berti
Kawahla
FUR
El Fasher
Geneina
Daju
Birqid
Ingessana
Baqqara
Nuba
DINKA
Uduk
Shilluk
Al-Ghazal
Sobat River
Ndogo
Kreish
Bviri
DINKA
Bongo
NUER
Murle
Azande
Baka
Moru
Bor
Avukaya
Mandari
Juba
Bari
Madi
Didinga
Kakwa
Kuku
Torit
Key
NUER Major ethnic group
Nuba Secondary ethnic group

While the name for the region comes from the Arabic *Bilad al-Sudan*, meaning "the Land of the Blacks," today only a little more than half of all Sudanese and South Sudanese are considered black Africans, while about 4 in 10 are said to be of Arab extraction. These broad distinctions—black African or Arab—which form a large part of the way many outsiders view Sudan's civil strife, conceal a much more complex situation. The historic Sudan region contains as many as 500 distinct ethnic groups, and with the exception of the Beja people—who for 5,000 years have kept to themselves in the hills alongside the Red Sea—few of these ethnic groups can be said to be wholly Arab or wholly black. This is especially true in the country of Sudan, where centuries of intermarriage have left it virtually impossible to distinguish people's ancestry on the basis of physical appearance.

EARLY HISTORY

Some 5,000 years ago, around the time Pharaoh Menes first united Upper and Lower Egypt and established Egypt's first dynasty, the ancestors of Sudan's Beja people settled in the Red Sea hills. To the west of the Beja lands, about 600 miles (965 kilometers) south of the evolving Egyptian civilization, smaller African states were also developing along the Nile River in a region of present-day northern Sudan and southern Egypt known as Nubia. As their power expanded, the Egyptians launched periodic raids into Nubia, seizing cattle and slaves. In the second millennium B.C., Egypt conquered the Nubian Kingdom of Kush and began appointing governors to administer the region and ensure a steady supply of goods Egyptian culture coveted, including gold, ivory, ebony, spices, gum arabic, tropical woods, incense, exotic animals, and African slaves.

Around 1075 B.C., the Egyptian state fell into a period of decline and disunity. Three centuries later, Nubians from the

Ruins of the Temple of Amun, constructed by Egyptian pharaohs around 1500 B.C. in Nubia, in present-day northern Sudan. In the eighth century B.C. the Nubian Kingdom of Kush conquered once-mighty Egypt.

Kingdom of Kush conquered their former overlords and, for about a century, ruled a reunited Egypt from their capital of Napata.

After a defeat by the Assyrians, the Kushites moved their capital farther south up the Nile River, to Meroë, about 600 B.C. There a new, distinctively African civilization evolved. Powerful, culturally advanced, and wealthy because of its control of regional trade, the Kingdom of Meroë flourished for hundreds of years.

THE COMING OF CHRISTIANITY

By the first or second century A.D., Meroë's power had begun to wane. Around the year 350, the kingdom was conquered by Axum, its neighbor to the east, in present-day Ethiopia. The king of Axum had recently converted to Christianity, and his conquest of Meroë introduced the faith into Nubia. Over the succeeding centuries, Christianity gained influence in Nubia, and in 580 it became Nubia's official religion.

Today's Coptic Christians in Sudan—who number perhaps 100,000 people nationwide and are concentrated in major towns and cities in the north—claim descent from these early Ethiopian Christian communities. Most of the remainder of contemporary Sudan's Christians—constituting 5 to 10 percent of the country's total population—live in the south. They belong to various Christian denominations that were introduced into the Sudan in the 19th and 20th centuries by European and American missionaries.

The early Sudanese Christian kingdoms that arose in and around Nubia, including Axum in Ethiopia and Dongola and Alwa in the Sudan, were militarily strong. In particular, they were feared for their fierce, swift-moving cavalry. However, beginning in the seventh century these kingdoms became progressively cut off from the rest of the Christian world—as well as from the ancient trade routes that would have ensured their continuing wealth—by the adherents of an expanding new faith.

THE ARRIVAL OF ISLAM

Around the year 610 the prophet Muhammad, a merchant in the town of Mecca, in present-day Saudi Arabia, is said to have received the first of a lifelong series of revelations from Allah, or God. The essence of those revelations was that human beings must submit to God's will. (The word *Muslim*, denoting a follower of Islam, comes from an Arabic term meaning "one who submits.") By the time of Muhammad's death in 632, most of the Arabian Peninsula had accepted the religion he founded: Islam.

Arab armies soon swept out of the Arabian Peninsula and spread their faith in all directions. By 640 Egypt had been conquered. This effectively isolated the Christian kingdoms of the Sudan from Byzantium (Constantinople), a major seat of Christianity and the center of the powerful Byzantine Empire.

Soon the Arabs were launching raids into Nubia. But in 652 the Arabs abandoned plans to conquer the region after ferocious Nubian resistance at Dongola. The two sides concluded a treaty whereby the Nubians would send 400 slaves to the Arabs annually, in return for which they would be given horses, cloth, and other items.

For several centuries afterward, relations between the Muslims and the Christian kingdoms of the Sudan remained strained but largely stable. Eventually the spread of Islam southward from Egypt and northwestern Africa and eastward from states alongside the Red Sea and around the Horn of Africa squeezed the Nubian Christian kingdoms. In the late 12th and early 13th centuries the Nubians sought alliances with—and in turn were asked for help from—Europe's Crusader princes, who were battling Muslims for control of the Holy Land. The Europeans were unable to help their African co-religionists, however.

In 1250 the Muslim Mamluk dynasty seized power in Egypt. The Mamluks—the descendants of slave warriors—began a relentless military campaign against the Christians of Nubia. In 1276 they captured the Dongolan king, Dawud, and forced his kingdom to convert to Islam. In 1317 Nubia's first Muslim king built the region's first mosque, in Dongola.

The smaller kingdom of Alwa—Nubia's last remaining Christian state—held out against the Muslims until the beginning of the 16th century. In 1504 it finally fell, and all of the Sudan came under the rule of two Muslim African sultanates: the Black Sultanate, ruled by the Funj sultan of Sennar, around the Nile area; and the Sultanate of Darfur, in the arid highlands to the west. The Funj derived its wealth mostly from its role funneling African slaves from further south to the northern slave markets in Egypt and the Middle East.

As it is illegal for Muslims to enslave fellow Muslims, conversion to Islam freed the ancient Nubians, the Beja, and other Africans who became Muslims from the bonds of slavery. However, among the unconverted neighbors of these Nilo-Saharan sultanates, the fear of being captured by slave traders was widespread, creating interethnic anxiety and deep-seated mistrust that became part of the folk memories of many African peoples, including the Dinka and Nuer in the Sudan.

THE BAGGARA

Around the time of the fall of Alwa in 1504, according to the people known today as the Baggara, their ancestors arrived in the Sudan from Arabia. They were Bedouin, nomadic Arabs of the desert. These newcomers eked out a living from herding cattle and some camels on the fragile arid soils of northern Sudan. The Humr, Messiria, Rizaygat, Shuwia, Hawazma, Ta'isha, and Habbaniya are all Baggara ethnic groups.

As they moved around in search of water and forage for their animals, the Baggara often crossed through the lands of farmers. Sometimes the settled communities welcomed the nomads with

A modern-day Baggara builds a fire. The Baggara, cattle-herding nomads, trace their ancestry to Bedouin who arrived in the Sudan from the Arabian Peninsula around the early 1500s.

open arms, but sometimes their arrival triggered arguments about access to water or grazing rights. Sometimes disputes between the nomads and the farmers descended into violent conflict, but usually such disputes were peaceably resolved by the traditional local authorities, the sultan or his nobles.

Sometimes Baggara men settled down among the farmers, took African wives, and ceased to be Baggara. Similarly, African farmers sometimes decided to give up the harsh life of cultivating desert soils, bought cattle herds, and opted for the nomadic life, eventually becoming accepted as Baggara.

Five centuries of these interactions virtually erased any physical difference between the Arab Baggara and the Nilo-Saharan

African farmers. Genetically they became virtually the same people. Even their histories became inextricably intertwined.

ARAB OR AFRICAN?

The Arab-ness of the Sudanese Baggara was—and continues to be—largely a matter of self-definition, a state of mind rather than a biological reality. The same is true of other Muslim ethnic groups in Sudan who consider themselves Arab. For example, the Birqid and Meidab of Darfur claim Arab descent but probably had Nile Nubian ancestors. Similarly, the 2 million Jaalayin Arabs—who today are settled farmers in the Nile Valley north of Khartoum—claim direct descent from the prophet Muhammad but are probably Nubian Africans. Their distinctive, decorative facial scarring (referred to as tribal marks) makes them visually indistinguishable from various ethnic groups in Nigeria who also identify themselves by facial scarring—hinting at a long-lost link.

Other ethnic groups in Sudan who claim a distant Bedouin tribal ancestor from Arabia are clearly of West African origin and arrived in Sudan relatively recently. From the Muslim kingdom of Bornu, located in present-day northeastern Nigeria, came people of Hausa origin (known as Takari) or Fulani origin (known as Fallata). Some arrived in Sudan as nomads and became Baggara; others settled in Sudan while en route to or from the hajj (the Muslim pilgrimage to Mecca). The descendants of these people, and later migrants from Nigeria's Borno State, today form about 6.5 percent of Sudan's population.

Because of the Muslim conquest, the conversion of indigenous peoples to Islam, and the migration of Muslims from other areas, Sudan today is predominantly a Muslim country. Nearly all of the country's 34 million people—Arab as well as African—are adherents of Islam.

By contrast, South Sudan's population of 11 million contains few Muslims. In addition to Christians, South Sudan contains numerous ethnic groups whose members follow a multitude of indigenous religions, some of them very ancient. The largest of these groups are the Dinka, who number about 4 million. Noted for their great height, the Dinka have links with other tall Nilo-Saharan speakers who trekked south in ancient times, such as the Maasai in Kenya.

COLONIAL RULE REINFORCES NORTH-SOUTH DIVISIONS

Over the centuries, as the cultural gulf between northern and southern Sudan widened, interregional antagonisms and fears also increased. A major factor was the slave trade. Muslims from the north—often the Baggara—periodically raided the south, seizing slaves, plundering, and terrorizing the inhabitants. British colonial rule would bring an end to slavery, but it would only cement the rift between northern and southern Sudan.

Numbering about 4 million, the Dinka are Sudan's largest non-Muslim ethnic group. These Dinka were photographed in the southern Sudanese town of Juba in September 2006.

Great Britain's interest in the Sudan stemmed largely from its proximity to Egypt and the Suez Canal. Completed in 1869, the waterway was a vital link between Britain and its most important and valuable colony, India.

In 1898—13 years after the British garrison at Khartoum was annihilated by a Sudanese Muslim leader known as the Mahdi—Anglo-Egyptian forces smashed the army of the Mahdi's successor, Abdullah et Taaisha. The British consolidated their control over the Sudan the following year. For the next five decades, the British would rule Sudan jointly with Egypt (except for the period 1924–1936, during which Egypt was excluded). This arrangement was referred to as the Condominium.

Britain's long rule in Sudan (1899–1956) is evident in this photograph of Khartoum, taken ca. 1936. The statue depicts Lord Horatio Kitchener, the British general who defeated the forces of the Sudanese Muslim leader Abdullah et Taaisha at the Battle of Omdurman.

To the British, the vast territory over which they gained control in 1899 seemed like two different countries, separated by language, culture, and history. In the north, following a pattern already established elsewhere in the British Empire, the British decided to leave the well-established Muslim administrations largely to themselves. In the southern areas, including Equatoria—the southernmost provinces bordering Uganda—the British ruled through "native administrations." Essentially this amounted to governing indirectly through cooperative indigenous leaders such as tribal chiefs.

By 1930 British administrators had crafted what was called the Southern Policy, which was supposed to prepare southern Sudan politically and economically for integration with the north. The Southern Policy's "closed-district ordinance" prohibited northerners from working in or even entering the south. Meanwhile, the Southern Policy sought to train southern boys for a future in the civil service. However, boys who qualified for secondary education were sent not to government schools in Khartoum but to schools in Kenya, Tanzania, and Uganda. This was largely because of the distance to Khartoum and because southerners spoke English or local languages rather than Arabic, the common tongue of the north. Unfortunately, the schools to which talented southern boys were sent tended to concentrate more on producing good Christians rather than good bureaucrats and administrators.

The British did virtually nothing to develop a sense of Sudanese national identity, which the people of southern areas had never had. They were Dinka, Shilluk, Nuer, Asholi, Bari, Azande, and a host of other ethnic groups first and foremost.

In 1946 the Southern Policy was suspended and its closed-door ordinances lifted as northern and southern Sudan were formally united. Northern merchants soon moved south, where they quickly came to dominate economic life. Furthermore, educated

British reforms in Sudan established an elected consultative body, the Legislative Assembly, in 1948. By 1951, when this photograph was taken, the members of the Legislative Assembly were demanding independence. Britain granted Sudan internal autonomy in 1953, and on January 1, 1956, the Republic of Sudan officially became an independent country.

northerners arrived to assume the government jobs for which southerners were unqualified—in large measure because Arabic was made the official language of administration.

The British granted Sudan internal autonomy in 1953. The following year, when 800 government administrative posts became available to Sudanese, only 6 of those posts were occupied by southerners.

CIVIL WAR

In August 1955, after general elections had been held ahead of independence on January 1, 1956, southern army officers in the Equatoria Corps—fearing that independence would bring complete domination by the north—mutinied. More than 300 people—260 of them northerners—died in the 1955 mutiny, which set the stage for a full-scale civil war.

Independent Sudan's civilian government proved unable to adequately address the concerns of southerners. In Khartoum the country's newly formed political parties squabbled incessantly; most represented the narrow interests of a single ethnic group rather than attempting to compromise for a more unified nation. In the south a similar situation existed, as ethnic differences prevented the kind of unity that might have given the region a greater voice nationally.

In 1958 Sudan's civilian government was overthrown by a military coup led by the army chief of staff, General Ibrahim Abbud. Abbud quickly abolished political parties, shut down the independent news media, and restricted the personal freedoms of Sudanese. He also confirmed southerners' long-standing fear of domination by the north when he filled almost all administrative and law enforcement posts with northerners.

Discontent in the south simmered. By 1962 many of the disparate southern factions had coalesced around the Anya Nya, a guerrilla group led by Joseph Lagu. Attacks by the Anya Nya prompted General Abbud to send the Sudanese army south to quash the rebellion.

As civil war raged in the south, however, opposition to Abbud's regime grew in the north. Massive demonstrations in Khartoum blossomed into the so-called October Revolution of 1964, which forced Abbud to step down. A transitional government was set up, and in 1965 general elections brought a permanent civilian government to power.

The return of democracy brought new opportunities for groups across the political spectrum, from the Sudanese Communist Party to the Islamic Charter Front. The latter group, inspired by Egypt's Muslim Brotherhood and led by Dr. Hassan al-Turabi, sought to establish a conservative Islamic government in Sudan. Meanwhile, the civil war in the south continued unabated.

In May 1969 a military coup led by Gaafar Nimeiry brought Sudan's latest experiment in democracy to an end. While he tolerated no dissent, banning all political parties except his Sudanese Socialist Union, executing dozens of Communists, and placing Hassan al-Turabi under house arrest for six years before exiling him to Libya, Nimeiry did work to end Sudan's civil war.

In 1972 Nimeiry's government and the Anya Nya signed a peace agreement in Addis Ababa, Ethiopia. The agreement unified the three southern provinces and granted the south political autonomy, including the right to establish a regional legislature and to collect its own taxes.

Nationally, Nimeiry decided to permit limited democracy, and conservative Islamist parties swept the board in two parliamentary elections. The Islamists were unhappy with the southern experiment in self-rule, fearing that it might undermine their drive toward the creation of a centralized, Islamic state in the north.

During the late 1970s, oil was discovered in Bentiu, in southern Sudan. But rather than bringing prosperity to the south, the oil would help re-ignite the north-south civil war. After Sudan's economy went into a period of decline, Nimeiry wanted the oil revenues from Bentiu to help pay Sudan's huge international debts. He reneged on the terms of the Addis Ababa agreement, rescinding the south's right to collect its own taxes. A new state was carved out of lands that historically belonged to the Nuer people of the Upper Nile. Unity State contained Sudan's main oil reserves, and Nimeiry argued that the move was necessary to protect the Nuer from any "greedy" appropriation of oil revenues by the Dinka majority. Southerners were highly skeptical of this explanation.

As the south's economic grievances mounted, political and religious tensions were added to the mix. In 1979 Nimeiry appointed Hassan al-Turabi, who had returned from exile in Libya two years earlier, to the position of attorney general. Turabi made no secret of his long-term political goal: transforming Sudan into an Arabized, Islamic state governed by Sharia (traditional Islamic law).

RESUMPTION OF FIGHTING

In 1983 a group of southern army officers based in the town of Bor mutinied. The officers, former commanders in Anya Nya, had been ordered north, in violation of the Addis Ababa peace agreement. Nimeiry soon declared that Islamic Sharia law would be imposed throughout Sudan and would apply not just to Muslims but to everyone, including Christians and followers of traditional African religions. After a decade-long respite, Sudan's civil war resumed. This time the fighting would rage on for 21 years.

Leading the southern rebels was Colonel John Garang, head of the Sudan People's Liberation Army (SPLA), the military wing of the new Sudan People's Liberation Movement (SPLM). Garang, a Dinka, believed that the south should have the right of self-determination. But, unlike other members of the SPLM, he opposed the secession of parts of the south along ethnic lines; he favored a united Sudan.

The government of Khartoum quickly sought to exploit ethnic differences, however. Nimeiry tried to recruit and mobilize a local Nuer militia calling themselves "Anya-Nya Two" to help defend their Bentiu area against the largely Dinka SPLA. Ultimately the Dinka and Nuer would spend years battling against each other in a war within a war; the two groups finally signed a peace agreement in 1999.

In 1985 Nimeiry was deposed in a bloodless coup. The following year, after general elections, a civilian coalition government was formed. Its efforts to bring about a cease-fire with the SPLA failed, and the civil war ground on.

The civilian government was overthrown in June 1989 by yet another coup, this one led by Brigadier Omar Hassan al-Bashir. A 15-member Revolutionary Command Council was set up to rule Sudan, with Bashir as its chairman. To broaden his base of support, Bashir allied with the National Islamic Front (NIF), led by Hassan al-Turabi. The NIF soon wielded considerable influence with the Revolutionary Command Council, and in 1991 Sharia law was introduced in northern Sudan.

Sudan's new rulers also brought a particularly ruthless approach to fighting the civil war. With the encouragement of Turabi, the government unleashed a newly formed paramilitary militia known as the Popular Defense Forces (PDF). Composed largely of Baggara, the PDF was ordered to wage a "jihad," or holy war, against the non-Muslims of the south. As Baggara raiders had done in centuries past, the PDF swept through the transitional zone between north and south—including southern Darfur, southern Kordofan, northern Bahr el Ghazal, and northern Blue Nile—killing, looting, and even seizing captives to be sold as slaves.

Eventually, the militiamen turned on Muslims as well. After the jihad had extended into the Nuba Mountains, countless small ethnic groups—many of them African Muslims—found themselves herded into so-called peace camps, ostensibly for their own protection. PDF raiders, meanwhile, took their land and possessions.

In 1993, with Sudan's civil war still raging, the Revolutionary Command Council was dissolved and Omar al-Bashir named president. Non-party elections held in 1996 confirmed Bashir as president. Hassan al-Turabi became speaker of Sudan's parliament, the National Assembly. The two men formed the National Congress Party in early 1999. But later in the year, Turabi introduced a bill into Sudan's parliament that would have curtailed the president's powers. Bashir responded by declaring a state of

Hassan al-Turabi (left) and Omar al-Bashir, photographed in December 1993. By the end of the 1990s, the two men would become political enemies.

emergency, dissolving the parliament, and forcing Turabi out of the National Congress Party.

THE CIVIL WAR WINDS DOWN

Turabi would go on to form another party, the Popular National Congress (PNC), which in February 2001 signed a memorandum of understanding with the southern SPLA rebels. Turabi also called on young Arab northerners not to fight in what he now said was a war for southern Sudan's oil. Bashir had his former ally arrested, but Turabi's advocacy of a resolution to the civil war was a hopeful sign.

In 2002 a ceasefire brought hope to the Nuba Mountains. There 100,000 people had died and 170,000 had been "resettled" during the brutal PDF jihad.

Later that year, Bashir and John Garang met to discuss peace. Two years of hard bargaining followed in neutral Kenya. In 2003

Displaced members of the Mundari ethnic group in a refugee camp outside Juba, 1986. Sudan's decades-long north-south civil war forced countless people from their homes and claimed the lives of more than 2.5 million people.

security arrangements were agreed to, and in 2004 agreement was reached over the sharing the oil revenues, power sharing, and administrative arrangements for the Nuba Mountains and southern Blue Nile areas.

Finally, on January 9, 2005, the Sudan People's Liberation Movement and the Sudanese government signed the Final Comprehensive Peace Agreement. The north-south civil war, which had claimed the lives of an estimated 2.5 million people and forced millions from their homes, was finally over.

In July 2005 more than a million ecstatic Sudanese, many of them displaced southerners, lined the streets of Khartoum to witness the arrival of their new vice president, John Garang. Tragically, on August 1, after barely a month in office, Garang was killed in a helicopter crash over southern Equatoria. Some southerners suspected that Garang's death was not an accident, and ethnic riots rocked Khartoum and other Sudanese cities for

Sudanese vice president Ali Osman Mohamed Taha (left) and rebel leader John Garang hold up a copy of the peace agreement ending the country's north-south civil war, January 9, 2005.

several days. Ultimately, however, the north-south peace agreement held, and Garang's deputy, Salva Kiir, succeeded him as vice president.

As part of the 2005 Comprehensive Peace Agreement, the south was granted a six-year period of autonomy as part of Sudan. This was to be followed by a referendum, or public vote, to determine whether the region would remain part of Sudan or break away to form an independent state. In January 2011, the people of South Sudan voted overwhelmingly in favor of secession. Independence was attained on July 9, 2011.

NEW ETHNIC CONFLICTS

Unfortunately, while the Comprehensive Peace Agreement seemed to resolve Sudan's long-running north-south civil war, grievances were festering in two other areas whose people felt marginalized by Sudan's government in Khartoum. In the east, alongside Eritrea, the Beja people launched a series of attacks against various Red Sea installations. Oil and tourism had been bringing a degree of prosperity to the area, but the Beja felt left out.

The situation was far more serious in the west of Sudan, in the province of Darfur. There, in early 2003, a brutal conflict began. By the end of 2006, the United Nations, which had attempted to send peacekeeping troops to the region, estimated that the conflict had claimed 450,000 lives and forced more than 2 million people from their homes in Darfur.

On the surface, it appeared that there was little to fight over in Darfur. The province is sparsely populated: with an area about equal to that of France, Darfur has only about 6 million inhabitants. Unlike other regions of Sudan, Darfur has few resources. In contrast to the civil war, which largely pitted Arab Muslims from the north against Christian and animist southerners, the combatants in Darfur are all Sunni Muslims.

Silhouetted by fire, a Darfurian rebel fighter with an automatic rifle watches the village of Chero Kasi burn, September 7, 2004. Beginning in early 2003, Arab militias known as Janjaweed—operating with the support of the Sudanese government—waged a brutal campaign against the settled African farmers of Sudan's western Darfur region. Through systematic rape, murder, looting, and the burning of villages such as Chero Kasi, the Janjaweed sought to drive the black farmers from Darfur.

While Darfur is home to more than 35 ethnic groups, the major divide is between those who define themselves as Arabs and those who define themselves as Africans. The former have traditionally pursued a nomadic, pastoralist lifestyle. The latter are predominantly (but not exclusively) settled farmers. A major cause of the Darfur conflict is competition between the two groups for suitable land and water in this dry region.

Frictions between settled farmers and nomads moving their cattle and camel herds across the land have existed for centuries. In recent years, however, these frictions intensified in Darfur because three decades of recurrent drought and the expansion of the Sahara Desert made adequately watered land—essential for farmers and nomadic pastoralists alike—increasingly scarce. Banditry by nomadic Baggara groups rose. The Khartoum government didn't help matters by attempting to bring the ancient administrative structures of Darfur, and the province's blend of Islam and traditional religions, into line with the rest of the north under a strict Islamist interpretation of Sharia law.

Beginning in the mid-15th century, Darfur had existed as an independent Muslim kingdom, the Sultanate of Darfur. Dominated by a black African ethnic group, the Fur (the word *Darfur* means "house of the Fur" in Arabic), the sultanate flourished in large part because of the slave trade. Baggara raiders captured slaves from non-Muslim African groups living across Darfur's southern borders, like the Dinka and Nuer. But it was Muslim African merchants who shipped the captives to the slave markets of Cairo along the so-called Forty Days' Road. And the Darfur Sultanate grew rich by taxing the slave trade.

By the early 1700s, the Darfur sultans were actively encouraging settlement in the area by Muslim scholars from around the Islamic world. Yet the form of Islam practiced in Darfur blended orthodox Islam and practices and beliefs drawn from traditional African religions.

Because it contained few resources and was located in an area of little strategic importance, powerful outsiders largely left the Darfur Sultanate alone. The Darfur Sultanate was one of only two indigenous states to survive Europe's late-19th-century "Scramble for Africa." (Ethiopia was the other.) Darfur's independence was only compromised when it decided to launch a jihad against the British to support its First World War ally, the Ottoman Empire. In 1916 Darfur's last sultan, Ali Dinar, was routed, and the British incorporated Darfur into Sudan. While the sultanate had officially come to an end, for practical purposes administration of this vast, inhospitable terrain was left with those who knew it best, the Darfur aristocracy.

Facing Mecca, a rebel member of the Justice and Equality Movement says afternoon prayers. Unlike the north-south civil war, which primarily pitted Muslims against Christians and animists, all the combatants in the Darfur conflict are Muslims.

DARFUR: AFRICANS AND ARABS

Today, Darfur's main black African groups include the Fur, who number around 750,000, and the Masalit, who number approximately 250,000. Both of these groups of settled farmers have figured prominently in the recent Darfur conflict. Another African ethnic group that has been deeply involved in the conflict, despite their smaller numbers, are the Zaghawa. Reflecting the complexity of the situation in Darfur, the Zaghawa are nomads rather than settled farmers like the Fur and the Masalit. They roam across the borders of Sudan and Chad with their cattle herds.

Inhabitants of Darfur who consider themselves Arabs—specifically the Baggara—often use the term *abid*, meaning "slave," in referring to the Fur, the Masalit, and the Zaghawa. The epithet is inaccurate, as historically these Muslim groups, while black, enjoyed a higher social standing and were themselves slave traders and slave owners.

DARFUR IN FLAMES

In March of 2003, two Darfur rebel groups—the Sudan Liberation Army (SLA) and the Justice and Equality Movement (JEM)—launched attacks against government soldiers and policemen. The SLA, led by Abdul Wahid Mohamed al-Nur, drew its support mostly from the Fur and Masalit. The JEM was inspired by Arab Muslim opponents of Omar al-Bashir's regime, including Hassan al-Turabi, but in Darfur its support on the ground came mainly from Zaghawa. The rebel groups' initial attacks on government forces came after months of increased Baggara raiding. But their grievances against the Khartoum government went beyond its failure to protect their lives and property from the Arab raiders. Among black residents a widespread perception existed that Khartoum ignored Darfur's economic development (for example, there is today only one short stretch of paved road in the vast province) and marginalized them politically. The people of Darfur desired a share of the nation's resources and a measure of autonomy, and they were inspired by the success of the south—albeit after a long and difficult struggle—in winning concessions from Khartoum.

In the wake of the first SLA and JEM attacks, the Sudanese government, most independent observers agree, armed, trained, and unleashed Baggara-dominated Arab militias known as Janjaweed ("devils on horseback"). The Janjaweed swept into Fur and Masalit villages—often after air strikes by the Sudanese military—and perpetrated nightmarish violence. They slaughtered village people indiscriminately, raped women and girls, looted, burned, and even seized captives as slaves—just as Baggara groups had done in bygone centuries.

The brutal tactics spurred many men in Darfur to take up arms, swelling the ranks of the SLA and JEM. But they also produced a flood of refugees, achieving in parts of Darfur what was clearly one of the objectives of the campaign: "ethnically cleansing" the province of Africans. This served the interests of the Arab nomads because it gave them access to good land for their livestock. It also served the interests of the Sudanese government, which sought not only to put down the Darfur rebels but also to align the province more closely with Khartoum's strict Islamist agenda.

During the years of fighting, there have been several ceasefire agreements in hopes of negotiating a peace, but none have lasted. The most recent came in February 2010, when the Justice and Equality Movement agreed to talks with the Sudanese government. However, the peace was broken when JEM accused the government of bombing a village, and said it would no longer negotiate with the regime.

NIGERIA: MODERN POLITICS OF ETHNIC ENTITLEMENT

With more than 170 million people, Nigeria is Africa's most populous nation. The West African country is blessed with vast reserves of oil and gas, along with other natural resources. Despite its human and material resources, however, Africa's giant has failed to thrive. The lives of millions of its citizens have been blighted by violence and crippled personal aspirations. At the root of these problems is poverty, viewed through the distorting prism of ethnicity.

Nigeria has more than 250 ethnic groups, split between followers of Christianity, Islam, and traditional African religions. Since 1980 the country has suffered about 250 serious conflicts, and almost all have pitted one ethnic community or tribe against another. (Nigerians freely use the word *tribe* to differentiate people.) More than 20,000 Nigerians are believed to have been killed, and over 3 million displaced from their homes, since 1999, when the country returned to civilian rule after a long period of military governments.

Nigeria's ethnic troubles are frequently complicated by religious differences exploited by Muslim and Christian leaders. Historical disputes, muffled and compounded during the period of British colonial rule, also echo in 21st-century grievances. But mostly ethnic conflict in modern Nigeria has as its root cause the distribution of scarce resources by the government. Often the conflict grows from controversy surrounding critical appointments of federal officials, local rulers, or political candidates who will control government resources. In many cases, it is charged, these appointments do not meet "federal character"—the constitutional stipulation, introduced in 1979, that is designed to spread government largesse fairly among Nigeria's ethnic groups. At the local level this ethnic controversy manifests itself in "indigeneity"—the question of which ethnic group first lived in the area—and the accompanying struggle for resources between *indigenes* (natives) and *non-indigenes* (settlers).

A Human Rights Watch report summarized the stakes in the following way:

> According to common understanding in Nigeria and as a matter of government policy, the indigenes of any given locality are those persons who can prove that they belong to the ethnic community whose ancestors first settled the area. Everyone else is considered a non-indigene, no matter how strong their ties to the communities they live in.
>
> State and local governments throughout Nigeria have enacted policies that discriminate against non-indigenes and deny them access to some of the most important avenues of socio-economic mobility open to ordinary Nigerians. In many states, non-indigenes are openly denied the right to compete for government jobs and academic scholarships, while state-run public universities subject non-indigenes to discriminatory admissions policies and higher fees. Instead of working to combat this discrimination, federal government policies have often served to legitimize and reinforce it.

Tragically, the more Nigeria tries to address the issue of ethnicity and indigeneity through structural reform of the state, affirmative action programs, and federal revenue allocation

Two residents of Onitsha, a city in southern Nigeria, gaze at the ruins of a mosque destroyed by a mob of Christians. In Nigeria, religious animosities frequently ignite cycles of sectarian violence, but it is the allocation of government resources among the country's more than 250 ethnic groups that presents the greatest challenge to maintaining peace.

formulas, the worse the problem gets as ethnicity becomes a more and more important determinant of economic and social opportunity. As a result, being a Nigerian citizen is fast becoming an abstract and irrelevant concept, while the only identity—the only "qualification"—that matters to many modern Nigerians is their ethnic origin. For many ordinary people, what matters then is obtaining a "certificate of indigeneity," which supposedly proves their ethnicity and origin. This certificate is the key that opens doors to education, land ownership, contracts, and employment.

NIGERIA'S THREE DOMINANT ETHNIC GROUPS

Nigeria is dominated by the triangular relationship between its three main ethnic groups: the Yoruba, who live in the southwest and are both Muslims and Christians; the Muslim Hausa-Fulani, who live across the north; and the Igbo (also spelled Ibo), who live to the east of the confluence of the Niger and Benue Rivers and are mainly Catholic Christians.

None of the three major ethnic groups is large enough to unilaterally dictate political terms to the others. Although exact counts are unknown, because Nigeria's national censuses have been unreliable due to political interference and corruption, the Yoruba and Hausa-Fulani are each believed to number around 35 million people, the Igbo roughly 28 million.

The majority of government revenues in Nigeria derive from oil. There is little tax revenue, agricultural export revenues have collapsed since independence in 1960, and wealth creation outside of the oil sector is minimal. With the exception of those living in the industrial and financial capital Lagos, almost everyone in Nigeria relies in one way or another on the trickle down of oil money, supplemented by subsistence farming. How the oil money is divided up and how it seeps through to ordinary citizens

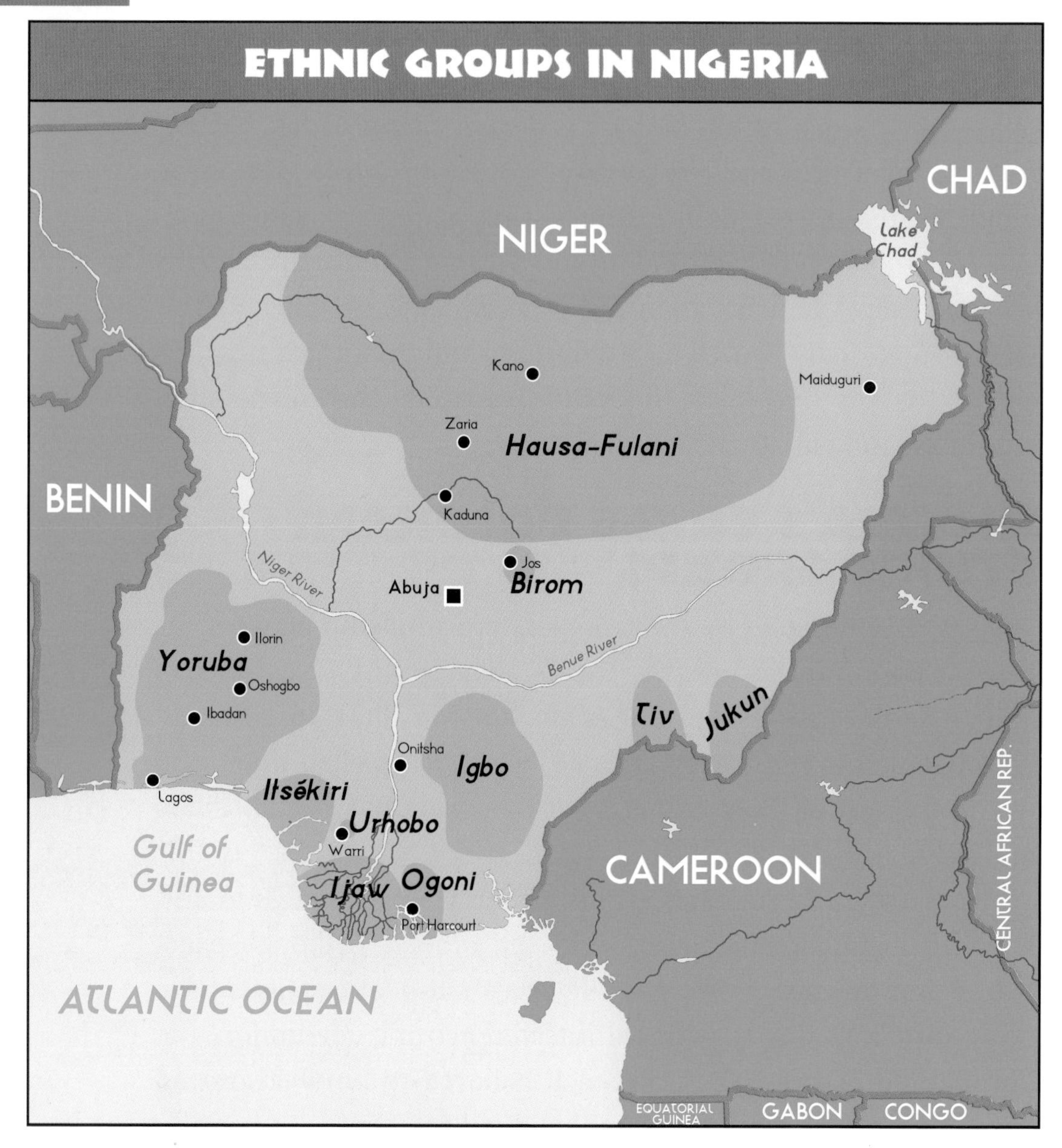

depends on area allocations, which are invariably appropriated by the dominant ethnic group. Dominance is decided on indigeneity, combined with numerical superiority in an area. Not surprisingly, historical scholarship and mapping boundaries have become contentious issues, frequently dissolving into violent dispute as researchers and surveyors attempt to answer fundamental questions about Nigerians: who are they, where are they, when did they settle there, and how many are there today?

BOUNDARIES

Great Britain acquired Lagos from a native king in 1861. Over the next half-century, the British expanded and consolidated their control, establishing various protectorates. In 1914 the British amalgamated their protectorates to create Nigeria.

Olusegun Obasanjo, a Yoruba and a Christian, was elected Nigeria's president in 1999 and reelected in 2003.

In 1939 three administrative areas were created: the mainly Hausa-Fulani Northern Region, the mainly Yoruba Western Region, and the mainly Igbo Eastern Region.

In the years following independence in 1960, new states were created in response to the complaints by ethnic minorities that their needs were being overlooked by the dominant ethnic group in each region. Today there are 36 states in Nigeria, and the number of local government areas (LGAs) has risen from 131 in 1963 to 774 in 2013. Most of these administrative areas have been created solely to give ethnic minorities one place in the country where they can be in the majority and claim federal revenues for their own people.

THE "DOUBLE MINORITY" PROBLEM

One result of the proliferation of LGAs and states is the creation throughout Nigeria of "double minority" situations—in which

A Fulani herder tends his cattle, central Nigeria, 2004. Followers of Islam, the Fulani—in combination with their Hausa co-religionists—constitute one of Nigeria's three dominant ethnic blocs.

an enclave of people whose ethnic group is large nationally find themselves isolated (and relatively powerless) in an area dominated by another ethnic group whose numbers nationally are small or even insignificant. For instance, in Plateau State, near the geographical center of Nigeria, the Hausa form a minority in the capital city, Jos, and are oppressed as non-indigenes by the Birom, a minority Christian ethnic group numbering perhaps only 300,000 nationally.

A similar situation exists in the conflict-riddled Niger River Delta, Nigeria's oil-producing area. The city of Warri, a major center of the oil industry, has been claimed by Itsekiri indigenes, leaving local non-indigene Urhobo and Ijaws (Nigeria's fourth largest ethnic group) as marginalized, disenfranchised, and impoverished minorities despite their far greater numbers nationally.

Taraba is a state on Nigeria's eastern border with Cameroon. It is the site of long-running battles between the local majority Jukun people—descendants of the warlike Kwararafa kingdom that terrorized Hausa states in the 16th to 18th centuries—and many minority non-indigenes, including Hausa farmers and Fulani cattle herders. The Tiv, Nigeria's seventh-largest ethnic group, who have their "own" state in neighboring Benue, are an especially unwelcome "settler" minority in next-door Taraba.

In all these instances the local majority indigenes want the non-indigenes to go home. Yet for many of the non-indigenes, home has been Jos, Warri, or Taraba for generations. And the

A funeral procession for nine Ijaw militants killed by government soldiers in the Niger Delta city of Warri. Although they represent Nigeria's fourth-largest group nationwide, Ijaws are "non-indigenes"—and hence disenfranchised and impoverished—in Warri.

constitution of Nigeria supposedly extends the same rights to all citizens to live wherever they choose, regardless of sex, religion, or ethnicity.

Not surprisingly, the double minority situation has resulted in bloodletting. Several thousand people have been killed in and around the cities of Jos, Warri, Taraba, and Lagos between 2001 and 2013, due to attacks by both Christians and Muslims. In 2009, an Islamic fringe group called Boko Haram, which was based in northeastern Nigeria, initiated a terror campaign that resulted in hundreds of deaths and did not end until its leader was killed by government soldiers. Boko Haram has continued to carry out sporadic attacks, and Nigerian Christians have responded in kind.

"TRIBAL" CONFLICT AND ETHNIC IDENTITY

Overarching ethnic allegiance is no guarantee against communal conflict. For example, the Yoruba meet virtually all the classic criteria for an ethnic group: shared language, ancestry, territory, and cultural and historical traditions. Yet for centuries Yoruba city-states such as Ibadan Ife, Illorin, and Oyo competed and sometimes went to war with each other, much like the city-states of ancient Greece. In many respects it was the colonial period—during which the British governed Yoruba areas as a single administrative unit—that forged a sense of solidarity among the Yoruba. The frequently fractured politics of recent years have, however, exposed divisions—which some observers characterize as "fundamental"—between Yoruba people. For instance, a newly created, wholly Yoruba state, Osun, in the western heartland of the Yoruba people has been plagued by violence between the indigenes of the Yoruba's ancient spiritual home, Ife, and non-indigene Yoruba, the Modakeke, who settled in the area in the late 19th century during a period of Yoruba civil war.

Likewise with the Igbo, there was little historical unity between the myriad village communities in the forests of eastern Nigeria. Archaeological remains of royal burials at Igbo-Ukwu, dated to the 9th and 10th centuries A.D., point to a sophisticated culture. However, there is little evidence of any other Igbo kingdom. Rather, there were dispersed clans, each one venerating its ancestral founders and accepting local, communal governance. In Chinua Achebe's classic novel, *Things Fall Apart*, he relates the mutual suspiciousness between Igbo clans and the ease with which colonialism found a foothold in the area: "The white man is very clever. He came quietly and peaceably with his religion. We were amused at his foolishness and allowed him to stay. Now he has won our brothers, and our clan can no longer act like one. He has put a knife on the things that held us together and we have fallen apart."

In 1999 Igbo homeowners in Lagos, worried about becoming caught up in fighting between rival Yoruba groups, identified their ethnicity with hand-painted signs.

In Nigeria, as in Sudan, the only cohesive ethnic groups in historical times were those that were bound together by Islam and its feudal infrastructure. These groups were all northerners: the Hausa, who were conquered and ruled by the nomadic Fulani; and the Kanuri, Nigeria's fifth-largest ethnic group, whose 4 million people share ancient roots with the Zaghawa of Chad and Darfur. Ninth-century Kanuri founded the Muslim Kanem-Bornu Empire around Lake Chad. It lasted for almost 1,000 years, controlled the trans-Saharan trade routes, and peaked in the late 16th century.

HISTORICAL JUSTIFICATIONS FOR MODERN ETHNIC GRIEVANCES

Among the people of the Middle Belt—the region that extends from east to west through the middle of Nigeria and that historically separated the cultures of the north and those of the south—history is a keen weapon in the arsenal of "indigeneity" arguments. Some ethnic groups in Plateau State claim to be the true natives of the area through unproven descent from Nigeria's earliest known civilization, the Neolithic Nok people, who lived in the area around 800 B.C. to A.D. 200. What is known is that northern Muslims—the Kanuri Kanem-Bornu Empire and, from A.D. 1000 onward, Hausa from the city-states of Kano, Zaria, Daura, Katsina, and Gobir—treated non-Islamic Middle Belt ethnic groups with contempt and as a huge source of potential slaves to be sent north along trans-Saharan trade routes to Arab slave markets. As in the Sudan, the experience left a bitter historical legacy and a reluctance to acknowledge the present-day rights of Hausa-Fulani residents in many Middle Belt states.

Despite the historical threat from the Muslim states to their north, Middle Belt minorities never fell under the direct rule of the Kanuri, Hausa, or Fulani until the British conquered Nigeria. The 1804–1812 jihad launched by Usman dan Fodio

(1754–1817) succeeded in establishing Fulani religious and political control of Islamic Hausa states, and in 1809 a new Hausa-Fulani multiethnic caliphate was created. It was headquartered in the remote northwestern desert state of Sokoto. But the jihad never completed its conquest of the non-Hausa peoples along the caliphate's southern borders. By the end of the 19th century the caliphate was crumbling and challenged from within by young Muslim radicals. In 1903, however, the British arrived and reinforced the sultan's rule.

Seeing the opportunity to use a preexisting administrative structure with a clear social hierarchy, the British colonialists allied with the conservative sultan, bolstered his ability to deal with dissidents, and arbitrarily placed unconquered, Middle Belt, non-Muslim people under feudal Muslim rule. A century later, some of the bloodiest ethnic battles—such as those in the western central state of Kaduna—have been between non-Muslim people, including the Atyap of Zangon-Kataf, and their Hausa neighbors. Both groups have probably coexisted in southern areas of Kaduna State since 1605. But the Atyap experience of being arbitrarily placed under the rule of the Muslim emir of Zaria—and their subsequent harsh treatment at the hands of their new Hausa rulers during colonialism—apparently hardened attitudes into an uncompromising stand about who is and is not a true "son of the soil"—an indigene—in 21st-century local government areas.

Kaduna city, an administrative center built by the British, has also seen appalling bloodshed. In 2000 the proposed extension of Islamic Sharia law to criminal matters sparked deadly clashes between Christians and Muslims, claiming the lives of at least 2,000 people. Two years later, the city again erupted in intercommunal violence, this time resulting in an estimated 250 killed. The spark was Muslim anger over the Miss World beauty pageant, which was to be held in Nigeria, and specifically a newspaper story about the pageant that Muslims claimed had insulted the prophet Muhammad. After Muslim youths attacked Christians and burned and looted Christian neighborhoods, Christians responded in kind.

Although Kaduna's conflicts are religiously based, deep ethnic resentments add fuel. A hundred years ago Christianity was widely embraced by ethnic groups oppressed under feudalism. Today many of the descendants of these converts believe they are discriminated against. This is because district heads must approve an application for a certificate of indigeneity before it is submitted to local government authorities—and district heads in Kaduna are appointed by the Muslim emir of Zaria. Christians complain that district heads have not been approving legitimate applications. Instead, they say, people with Christian names have been palmed off with meaningless "certificates of settlership," allegedly on the orders of the emir. The implications of this administrative fiat are disastrous for many young people. One young man told Human Rights Watch in 2005, "If you are given a settlership form you are not an indigene of that area, so you are not eligible for any quota—it could be for a job or for admission [to higher education, the civil service, or the military]. You are completely disqualified from everything."

The examples noted above describe ethnic conflicts where the assertions of indigeneity or non-indigeneity are based almost entirely on periods of history that are poorly documented, in addition to being at least a century, if not several centuries, distant. The arbitrariness of colonial decision making with respect to the establishment of boundaries and governance aggravated many preexisting communal disagreements, but by and large people from different ethnic groups coexisted peaceably and often intermarried during colonial times. It is the post-independence divvying up of state spoils that has rejuvenated ethnic protectionism as Nigerians ask, "Who is getting the most?" and "Who is

In November 2002 three days of deadly violence convulsed the northern Nigerian city of Kaduna after Muslim mobs—angered by the upcoming Miss World beauty pageant—attacked Christians, who quickly retaliated. In this photo a house burns in the foreground while a roving gang can be seen along the rails in the background.

responsible for my poverty?" and their leaders reply, "The others. The strangers."

NEW SETTLERS AND NEW PROBLEMS

In southern Nigeria, colonial rule was direct and Western education was introduced. The result was that many southerners, especially Igbo and Yoruba, spread themselves around the country, filling a large proportion of the skilled and professional jobs demanded by the 20th-century economy. In the north the conservative emirs ensured that education was limited to boys attending Quranic schools, where they memorized scripture in

Arabic. Too late the Hausa-Fulani aristocrats realized the importance of a liberal education if their people were to compete with the southerners in the modern economy.

The British allowed the northern emirs to limit housing for southern settlers to areas called *sabon garis* (meaning "strangers' quarters"). By contrast, throughout Nigeria the colonial administrators and missionaries built themselves comfortable homes in government residential areas (GRAs) away from the natives. This colonial segregation had negative consequences. First, in the north, Nigerians were prevented from intermingling with one another outside of work—and northern women were largely kept in seclusion, apart from neighbors who were strangers and out of the workforce. Second, when independence came, the new Nigerian ruling class appropriated the domestic trappings of the British administrators, with the perception that ruling a country is primarily about state-provided personal entitlements and perks.

In the new Nigerian order, the key to advancement was not individual merit but ethnicity ("federal character"). Sadly, the scientists, engineers, and entrepreneurs whose genius formed the bedrock of the industrial revolution and modern society in every other country were frustrated and neglected in the new Nigeria, whose rulers preferred to buy in such skills from overseas rather than appoint non-indigenes from outside their home areas.

The bankrupt, unaccountable portioning out of the prizes of self-government after 1960 precipitated the fall of the first republic in 1966, when six idealistic young army officers unsuccessfully attempted to seize power in a coup designed to end the corruption. Two Sokoto aristocrats—the prime minister, Sir Abubakar Tafawa Balewa, and the powerful leader of the north, Ahmadu Bello—were killed along with their Yoruba ally, the Western Region premier Samuel Akintola, who had grabbed power in a rigged election. After the failed coup, what was left of the federal cabinet surrendered power to General John

Aguiyi-Ironsi, thereby opening the door to 28 years of military rule in Nigeria and paving the way for civil war.

BIAFRA AND AFTER

The coup was interpreted as ethnically motivated. Five of the six young officers were Igbo. Most of the coup's victims were northerners, and none was Igbo. General Aguiyi-Ironsi, who assumed power as Nigeria's head of state, was Igbo.

Aguiyi-Ironsi attempted to run the country as a unified entity without regard to ethnic balancing. Seven months after he took power, however, he was killed in a counter-coup that returned northerners to power. The massacring of Igbos in the *sabon garis* of northern towns and cities and the wave of southern refugees flooding south to safety triggered the secession from Nigeria of the Igbo-dominated Eastern Region. In May 1967 Colonel Emeka Ojukwu, the leader of the Eastern Region, proclaimed the independent Republic of Biafra. But Biafra secessionists also seized neighboring oil-producing areas of Nigeria that were not Igbo homelands, and the Nigerian army immediately launched a "police action" to recover these valuable lands and to reunite the country.

General Yakubu Gowon was head of Nigeria's military government from 1966 to 1975. He succeeded in putting down the attempt by Igbo to create an independent Biafran state.

For two and a half years civil war raged on both sides of the Niger River, bringing devastation to Igbo areas on the Niger's east bank and also to west bank areas called the Mid-West, home to Edo people of the old Benin Empire, Ijaws, and other southern minorities. Some Igbo leaders had calculated that Yoruba nationalists would support Biafra's

Two and a half years of civil war followed the secession of Nigeria's predominantly Igbo Eastern Region, which proclaimed itself the independent Republic of Biafra on May 30, 1967. As many as 2 million Nigerians died as a result of the war. Like these starving children, most were civilians.

cause to advance their own aspirations for an independent Yoruba region. To their surprise, however, Yoruba nationalists refused to join them and instead backed the army offensive to keep Nigeria together. Between 1 million and 2 million people died as a result of the war, which ended in 1970. Most were civilians who succumbed to starvation or disease.

The end of the war brought attempts at ethnic reconciliation. The government promised a "no victor, no vanquished" peace formula and initiated massive reconstruction programs, which were financed by colossal oil revenues. But Nigeria's 12 states were governed as personal fiefdoms by military governors appointed by General Yakubu Gowon, who had led the Nigerian federal forces through the civil war. Unaccountable, like its civilian predecessors, this new military regime was toppled by Brigadier General Murtala Muhammed, a northerner with a reputation for probity and discipline. He was widely welcomed as a savior by Nigerians of all ethnic groups—demonstrating that, given the right political leadership, ethnic differences become politically irrelevant even in a country as ethnically diverse as Nigeria.

Murtala Muhammed was credited with bringing order to Nigeria's social chaos. He created seven more states to allow minority groups more say in government and made the decision to move the Nigerian capital from Yoruba Lagos to Abuja, a central location deliberately chosen as neither Hausa-Fulani, nor Yoruba, nor Igbo. Murtala Muhammed eschewed the trappings of power, a low-profile approach that won him the respect of ordinary Nigerians. However, in February 1976, six months after taking power, he was assassinated as part of a coup attempt.

General Olusegun Obasanjo, a Yoruba and Murtala Muhammed's deputy, took over as head of state and executed 30 of the coup plotters. In 1979 Obasanjo fulfilled Murtala Muhammed's plan, handing over power to a civilian government after national elections.

Unfortunately, the civilian rulers resumed their plunderous ways. Public disenchantment with the corruption was widespread. In 1983, when General Muhammed Buhari, another northern aristocrat, led a bloodless coup that overthrew the government, most Nigerians approved. But the public mood was decidedly different by the following year, when Buhari's military regime launched its so-called War Against Indiscipline. Though its goals included cleaning up corruption and promoting law and order, many Nigerians resented the campaign's heavy-handedness. Human rights abuses proliferated.

In 1985 Buhari was deposed by his deputy, General Ibrahim Babangida. Babangida, another northerner, ruled as the head of a military regime but also assumed the title of president. He promised to step down by 1990. Most Nigerians initially regarded the general as a welcome change, but the goodwill gradually evaporated in the face of regional and ethnic squabbling and, ultimately, rioting. Babangida responded with an ironfisted crackdown, banned political parties, and announced that he would remain in office past 1990. He would rule Nigeria until 1993.

That year the military approved just two political parties to compete for power, provided they each met stringent ethnic balancing requirements that demonstrated multiethnic support in every state of Nigeria. In elections that were internationally acclaimed as free and fair, Chief Moshood Abiola, a Muslim Yoruba multimillionaire philanthropist, won the presidency with widespread popular support in both the north and west of the country.

Chief Moshood Abiola casts his ballot in Nigeria's 1993 presidential elections. Though he won the vote, Abiola was prevented from assuming the office of president by the country's former military ruler, General Ibrahim Babangida.

Inexplicably, Babangida annulled the election, citing fraud. Babangida appointed an unelected interim government headed by a Yoruba bank chairman, Chief Ernest Shonekan. The country ground to a halt as unions called a general strike in support of Chief Abiola. A Hausa general, Sani Abacha, took the opportunity to seize power. The army crushed pro-democracy demonstrations with great loss of life; jailed Chief Abiola, General Obasanjo, and human rights leaders such as Dr. Beko Ransome-Kuti; and muzzled critical journalists. Abacha created further outrage by executing the Nigerian author Ken Saro-

Wiwa, a leading activist for the rights of the Ogoni people, a small ethnic minority. Despite the fact that large oil deposits had been found beneath their ancestral homeland, the Ogoni remained desperately poor, and their land was severely polluted.

In 1998 Abacha died. He was succeeded by Major General Abdulsalami Abubakar. One month later Chief Abiola, who was still imprisoned, also died. The Yoruba felt profoundly cheated out of "their turn" in government.

Before Abacha's brutal rule, Nigerians joked that since the civil war there had been a two-party state: the civilians and the generals. After Abacha the prospect of military government was repugnant. General elections were quickly organized. Behind the scenes, Nigerian leaders agreed that the next civilian president should be a Yoruba to appease the outrage of 1993, and in 1999 two Yoruba presidential candidates faced each other in new polls. The winner was the former general Olusegun Obasanjo. In 2003 Obasanjo was reelected.

With the approach of the 2007 presidential elections, the ethnic maneuvering among Nigeria's wealthy ruling elite once again came to the fore. Having "given" the presidency to the south in 1999 and 2003, many powerful northerners believed it should return to the north. Many Igbo complained that after providing independent Nigeria's first president, Dr. Nnamdi Azikiwe, few of their group had enjoyed federal power since the civil war. Igbo had been courted as a junior political partner in various power-brokering arrangements with Yoruba and Hausa-Fulani politicians since 1970. But now, many Igbo insisted, their turn at the top was long overdue. A new Igbo nationalist movement, the Movement for the Actualization of the Sovereign State of Biafra (MASSOB), was formed to redress perceived discrimination against Igbo in the federal order.

However, 21st-century politics in Nigeria has moved beyond simple power-sharing arrangements between the big three ethnic

Nigerian President Umaru Yar'Adua meets UN Secretary-General Ban Ki-moon, 2007. Yar'Adua's poor health led to the appointment of his vice president, Goodluck Jonathan, as acting president in February 2010. Yar'Adua was to regain his executive position once he returned to full health; however, he died in May 2010.

groups. In the run-up to the election a variety of new ethnically based political units gave voice to the previously ignored 40 percent of the population who are not Yoruba, Hausa-Fulani, or Igbo. Ultimately, Umaru Yar´Adua, a Fulani Muslim from Katsina State in northern Nigeria, was elected president in 2007. This marked the first time in Nigerian history that one civilian leader had peacefully succeeded another.

The new president moved to restore stability in the Niger Delta, where interethnic fighting, pipeline sabotage, and a wave of kidnappings targeting employees of foreign oil companies had affected the country's oil production. Although Yar'Adua gained some ground, peace was not entirely secured. In 2008, a series of strikes and attacks on oil pipelines in the region cut Nigeria's production in half. Yar'Adua responded with a campaign to offer amnesty to warlords and their followers in exchange for their disarmament in 2009. The government managed to decommission a large number of weapons, yet as charges of corruption and mismanagement of the amnesty mounted, hopes for a permanent peace faded.

Further derailing the peace was a serious leadership vacuum resulting from the president's poor health. A chronic kidney condition incapacitated him from late 2009 until his death in May of the following year. By that point, Nigeria's parliament had appointed Vice-President Goodluck Jonathan, a Christian from Bayelsa State in the Niger Delta region of is a state in southern Nigeria, to finish Yar'Adua's presidential term.

Goodluck Jonathan, an ethnic Ijaw, became the first member of his tribe to serve as president of Nigeria. He was elected to a full term as Nigeria's president in 2011.

One of the first challenges Jonathan faced as leader was dealing with more attacks on oil facilities in the Niger Delta. In November 2010, a militant group known as the Movement for the Emancipation of the Niger Delta (MEND) called off a yearlong ceasefire. In March 2011, the group claimed that a bomb explosion on an oil platform in southern Nigeria was the start of a major bombing campaign.

In April 2011, a national election was held in which Goodluck Jonathan was elected to a four-year presidential term. Immediately after the election, riots broke out in the predominantly Muslim north. Muslim supporters of Jonathan's unsuccessful challenger, Muhammadu Buhari, attacked churches, homes, and police stations. The violence sparked counterattacks by Christians. Since the, the violence has continued and the country remains dangerously volatile.

5 HUTUS AND TUTSIS: GENOCIDE IN RWANDA

For 100 days between April and July 1994, an estimated 800,000 people were shot, hacked, clubbed, burned, blown up, impaled, buried alive, drowned, and tortured to death in Rwanda. Most of the victims were Tutsis who died at the hands of their Hutu countrymen simply because they were Tutsis. But up to 50,000 Hutus were also murdered because they opposed the government or because their consciences stopped them from killing their Tutsi spouses, relatives, neighbors, friends, and coworkers.

(Opposite) A human skull sits on the altar of the Catholic church in Ntarama, Rwanda, mute witness to the horror that occurred there in April 1994, when an estimated 5,000 Tutsis were massacred by Hutus. The church is now a memorial to the victims of the Rwanda genocide.

For decades before and the decade after the genocide, Rwanda—a tiny, utterly poor, spectacularly beautiful mountain kingdom of 8 million to 9 million people—was the epicenter of many regional crises. They were political crises that needed political solutions, but for too long too many actors in the unfolding tragedies played up the ethnic dimension. Only the Tutsi-led Rwandan Patriotic Front (RPF), made up of 60 percent Tutsis and 40 percent Hutus, tried to

move beyond simplistic ethnic explanations for the bloodletting—and move on to creating a modern state that can deal with grievances long before people are moved to kill one another over them.

There was evidence in Rwanda to support all three mainstream explanations for the ethnic conflict. First, there was a centuries-long history of feudal relations between the Tutsi aristocracy and Hutu farmers. Second, appalling, unthinking, racist exacerbation of Tutsi-Hutu differences occurred under German and Belgian colonial rule. And third, the post-independence constitutional provisions couldn't resolve ethnic conflict, especially under the dictatorial rule of hard-line Hutu nationalists who exaggerated ethnic differences to create Tutsi scapegoats for all social ills.

Today, decades after the catastrophic events of 1994, some scholars have suggested an alternative explanation: that the genocide was caused principally by economic factors. Hutu leaders, according to this line of thinking, exploited ethnic grievances to preserve their economic status—and found a receptive audience in Rwanda's impoverished people.

BACKGROUND

Rwanda, Africa's most densely populated country, is home to two major ethnic groups: the Hutus, who make up about 85 percent of the population, and the Tutsis, who make up about 14 percent. The remaining 1 percent are Twa, formerly known as Pygmy people. These percentages haven't changed much over the past few centuries. Even the massacre of up to 45 percent of the Tutsis within Rwanda in 1994 failed to alter the ethnic balance significantly, as the establishment of the post-genocide RPF government encouraged exiles and refugees from previous ethnic purges, many of them Tutsi, to return home with their children and grandchildren.

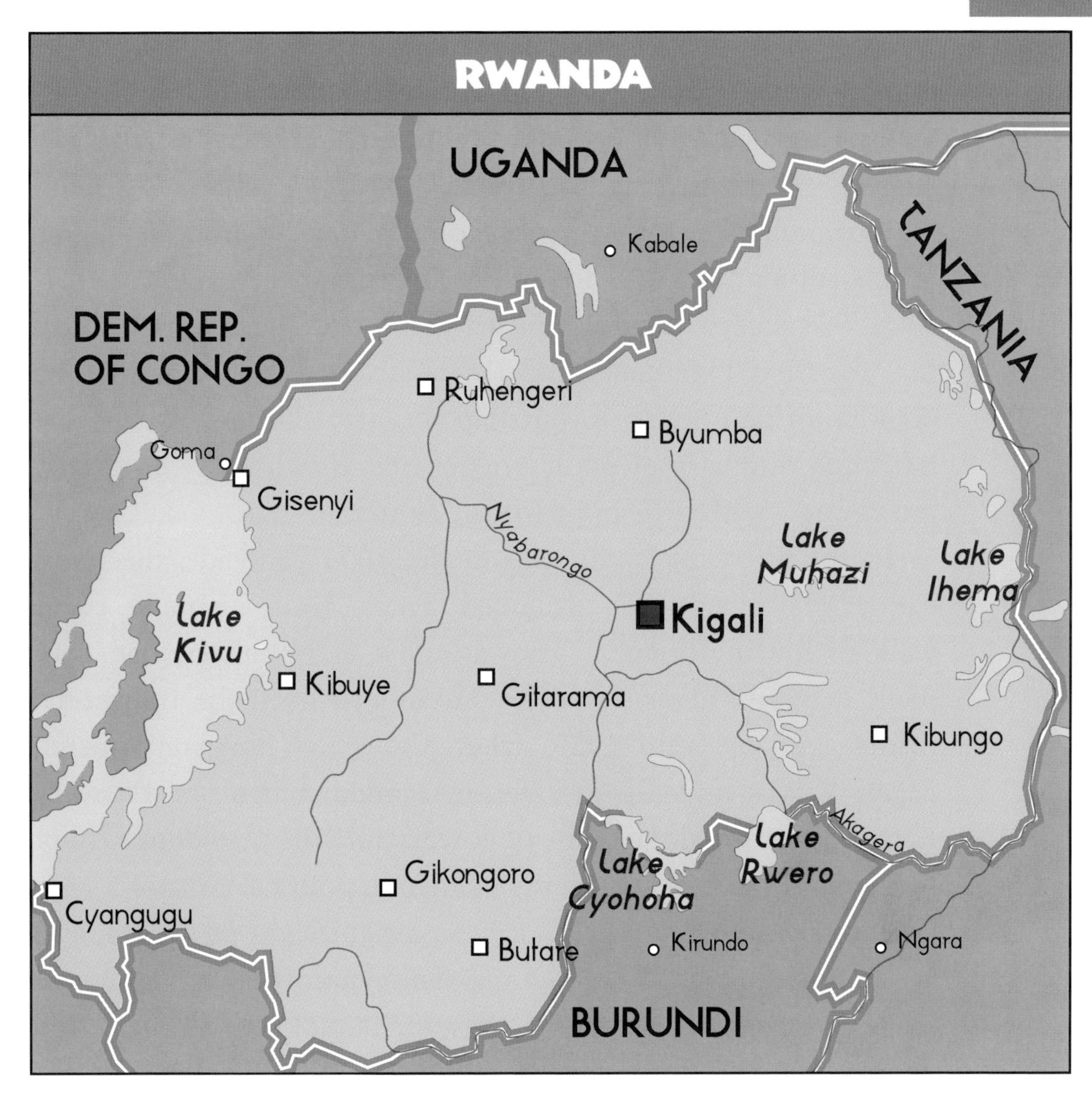

The 1994 genocide uprooted about a million people within Rwanda and sent an additional 2 million people, both Hutus and Tutsis, fleeing across borders into Uganda to the north, Tanzania to the east, Tutsi-ruled Burundi to the south, and the Democratic Republic of Congo (then called Zaire) to the west. This massive movement of people triggered humanitarian crises and placed considerable economic stress on Rwanda's already poor neighbors. It destabilized Zaire, which became the Democratic Republic of the Congo (DRC), then helped spark a brutal regional war in the DRC.

There is no denying that poverty formed the backdrop for the human catastrophe in Rwanda. During the late 1980s and early 1990s, the country's economy suffered a precipitous decline. Particularly devastating was the collapse in world prices for coffee, Rwanda's main source of income. Compounding the effects of this downturn was Rwanda's overreliance on agriculture: about 95 percent of the country's workers depended on agriculture for their livelihood, and Rwanda's large and fast-growing population had begun to outstrip the available farmland. This left large numbers of poor, uneducated Rwandans—especially the young—with little hope for the future.

In the 30 years leading up to the 1994 genocide, the Hutu majority systematically excluded Tutsis from virtually every walk of life in Rwanda. They became marginalized and very poor. It wasn't always so. The Tutsis had been the traditional ruling class up until 1959, when the Tutsi king, or *mwami*, Kigeri V, was forced into exile in Uganda. But it wasn't every Hutu who enjoyed the fruits of power; only the president's inner circle really benefited from the change in political control.

For centuries there had not been a significant power struggle between Hutus and Tutsis. As in many countries, however, the seeds of ethnic conflict were present. It took the German and Belgian colonial authorities to germinate them, but it was the Rwandans themselves who watered the seeds of hatred and brought them to bitter harvest.

ORIGINS OF HUTU, TUTSI, AND TWA

The Twa (or Batwa) were the original occupants of the Great Lakes region of East and Central Africa, which includes Rwanda. They have been progressively marginalized ever since the first Bantu people (the Hutus in Rwanda) settled the misty mountains more than 1,500 years ago. Recently the Twa of

Nyungwe Forest have been displaced yet again through the creation of a new military zone, while the Twa in the Parc des Volcans, of *Gorillas in the Mist* cinematic fame, have been moved out to make a sanctuary for mountain gorillas and a national park to bring in tourism and much-needed foreign exchange. Their plight has attracted international concern.

When the ancestors of the Tutsis—cattle-herding invaders of mixed Nilotic and Cushitic origin—arrived from the distant Ethiopian hills, far to the north, they found 15th-century Rwanda and neighboring Burundi peopled by Bantu farmers, the Hutus. They adopted the local language, often married local women, and developed a common culture and set of beliefs.

A Tutsi tends his cattle. In Rwanda cattle ownership, rather than racial heritage, traditionally determined whether a person was considered a Tutsi or a Hutu.

Some of the invaders even took wives from the forest-dwelling Twa people—who became "Tutsis," a distinction that reflected social and economic position, not racial origin. Cattle ownership marked a man's wealth, and the wealthiest cattle owners were the Tutsis. Some Hutus also kept cattle, and those who became wealthy enough could also become known as Tutsis.

Among the Tutsis an aristocratic class emerged around a royal clan. These people mixed less with the Hutus, and many retained the slim, tall features of their northern ancestors. However, the majority of Tutsis assimilated with the Hutus, and the two groups became virtually indistinguishable. Collectively they became known as Banyarwanda and spoke the same language, called Kinyarwanda in Rwanda and Kirundi in Burundi. Today the Banyarwanda are spread over Uganda and the Democratic Republic of the Congo. They are close relatives of the Banyankole and Bakiga in Uganda and the Barundi in Burundi.

The further away a person traveled from the royal court in central Rwanda, the less likely that person would be to encounter Rwandans distinguishing themselves as Hutu or Tutsi. Within the Banyarwanda diaspora, division into Hutu and Tutsi lost its significance in the outer reaches. The inhabitants of an island in Lake Kivu, a half hour's canoe paddle from the Rwandan shore, knew only of the "Badusi"—as they called Rwandans. The independently minded people of the northwest region—whose descendants would rule Rwanda from 1973 to 1994—felt little affinity with the feudal society around the Tutsi court. They were even sometimes known to identify themselves as Kiga or Bakiga, Banyarwanda who migrated into southern Uganda in the mid-19th century.

As the Banyarwanda consolidated under the rule of a succession of kings dating from the late 16th century—when a Tutsi prince was said to have forged a blood oath with a Hutu diviner to create a unified kingdom—the divisions into Hutu and Tutsi came to represent the poor and the successful respectively. Successful Hutu elites would merge with the Tutsis, becoming Tutsi.

The court of the mwami, or king, developed an elaborate court culture where the Tutsis "do no manual work and have leisure to cultivate eloquence, poetry, refined manners and the subtle art of being witty and drinking hydromel with friends," according to a French anthropologist writing in the 1950s. The coronation of every new mwami would be accompanied by a lengthy recitation of the royal genealogy, starting with the new king and going back in time to Muntu, the mythical father of all humankind.

COLONIALISM

By the late 19th century Mwami Kigeri Rwabugiri, king between 1860 and 1895, was in the final stages of expanding his state to include smaller Hutu kingdoms. He appointed two provincial chiefs, who were authorized by the royal court to select new hill chiefs. These hill chiefs replaced local rulers whose positions were inherited. Ethnicity became an issue, as the court-appointed chiefs tended to be Tutsis and the rulers they replaced Hutus. By the 1880s, using firearms imported from East Africa, Rwabugiri was raiding deep into southern Uganda and northwestern Tanzania, mainly for cattle. In 1894 he received the first Europeans to reach Uganda. He died the following year, leaving the Kingdom of Rwanda at the height of its power.

In 1890 the newly unified kingdom nominally became part of German East Africa, linked together with Burundi as Ruanda-Urundi. It is not recorded whether the old mwami realized his kingdom had become a German colony. But in due time a handful of administrators and missionaries arrived to colonize and "civilize" Rwanda. They found a highly organized state with a centralized military structure. After a power struggle between

Heinrich Albert Schnee (left) and Paul von Lettow-Vorbeck, who were responsible for the administration of German East Africa, ca. 1915. Following Germany's defeat in World War I, authority in the area that now makes up Rwanda and Burundi passed to Belgium under a League of Nations mandate.

Rwabugiri's sons, the new mwami, Yuhi IV Musinga, ruled from 1896 to 1931. He ushered in the colonial period by securing German backing in 1898 to subdue the obstinate Hutus, who didn't like the recent changes. By 1912 resentment in northern areas had grown into a full-fledged rebellion, which was put down by German forces acting on behalf of Mwami Musinga.

While the colonial authorities—just five German officials in 1913—were backing the Tutsi court, the missionaries had been scattered to distant places as far away from the court as possible. There the Catholic White Fathers found the poor and the disenfranchised, who eagerly received Christ's message of salvation. Converts were almost uniformly Hutu.

East Africa saw fierce fighting between the colonial powers during the First World War. At the close of the conflict, the Germans were displaced by the Belgians, who ruled Ruanda-Urundi first through a mandate from the newly established League of Nations and later, from 1924 to 1962, as a Trust Territory. In effect the area was administered as part of its huge western neighbor, the Belgian Congo (now the Democratic Republic of the Congo). The Belgians worsened social divisions by backing the mwami's rule. They established schools in the capital, Kigali, to produce the cadre they would need for colonial administration, but in the mid-1920s restricted entry to Tutsi boys only. The Belgians preferred the slim Tutsis, whose appearance seemed more "European" and whom they could relate to as existing "natural" rulers of Rwanda with a sophisticated court culture. Education of the Hutus remained in the hands of the White Fathers until 1929. That year the missionary priests spectacularly "changed sides" and began supporting the Tutsis after being allowed back into the capital after 30 years championing the Hutu cause in the Rwandan wilderness.

This early educational divide—a secular, elite education for the Tutsis and a missionary, Catholic education preaching salvation for the poor and oppressed for the Hutus—would have dire consequences in years to come. The process of ethnic differentiation was compounded when, in 1933, the Belgians introduced identity cards designating bearers as Twa, Hutu, or Tutsi. Despite the fluidity of ethnic distinctions in Rwanda, the identity card system set

A Rwandan identity card. First introduced in 1933 by the Belgian colonial administration, identity cards included the bearer's ethnic group.

ethnicity—for Rwandans at the time and for future generations—according to the ethnicity of a person's father. When the identity cards were introduced, the head of the household had to own more than 10 cows to qualify as Tutsi.

In 1931 the Belgians deposed the old king, Mwami Musinga. He had become disenchanted with his colonial backers and was unable to work with his subordinate chiefs. The Belgians replaced Musinga with one of his sons, Mutara III Rudahigwa, who had been baptized "Charles." Willing to operate within the colonial framework, the new king was prepared to advance Catholics to posts of power in preference to people who followed traditional African religions. Nevertheless, to the Hutu oppressed majority, Mutara III still symbolized Tutsi supremacy. Tutsi collaboration with the Belgians, especially as collectors of taxes, executioners, and enforcers of brutal punishments like amputations, was hard to forget.

INDEPENDENCE

After the Second World War, Belgian efforts to raise the status of the Hutus were too little and too late. Democratic reforms included the phasing out of feudal practices, including Hutu entitlements to using Tutsi cattle or land in exchange for services rendered to the Tutsi landlord (often forced labor). In 1954 the mwami oversaw a redistribution of land between Hutus and Tutsis, making him many enemies and few friends. Rwandan "feudalism" wasn't binding on the laboring Hutu class in the way that happened in European serf societies. Significant numbers of Hutus had already left the land to work in the mines of the Belgian Congo or in the cotton plantations of British Uganda. Many who did stay to cultivate the land began growing coffee, a lucrative cash crop. The coffee growers and the returning migrants formed a new rich class of Hutus, while the traditional Tutsi rulers were growing poorer despite owning cattle.

A second potential route of Hutu social advancement was through the Catholic Church. Hutu seminarians, exposed to the Christian ideals of equality and social justice, found to their growing resentment that their Tutsi colleagues were "more equal than others" and in many cases despised their Hutu brothers, which spawned a new political consciousness among the Hutu seminarians. Hutus who had received a mission education likewise found that they were discriminated against in the civil service, where they were restricted to the lowest rungs of the hierarchy.

In 1957 the Hutu Manifesto was drawn up by nine Hutu leaders, including a journalist named Grégoire Kayibanda. While

Hutu nationalist Grégoire Kayibanda, the primary author of the Hutu Manifesto, served as Rwanda's president from 1962 to 1973.

it demanded an end to feudal and other discriminatory practices and institutions, it also called for identity cards to remain as a means of monitoring the ethnic situation. Two new parties were formed to represent the Hutu majority. One was the ethnically based Mouvement Social Muhutu (MSM), led by Kayibanda, the Hutu former editor of the Catholic newspaper *L'Ami*. The other party, the Association pour la Promotion Sociale de la Masse (APROMOSA), was class based.

By 1959 Kayibanda's party, now called Parti du Mouvement et de l'Emancipation des Bahutu (PARMEHUTU), had grown to be the biggest political party in the country. It drew support from Hutus living in the south and center of the country. Also prominent among the Hutu leaders were northwesterners.

The year 1959 marked the beginning of the Hutu social revolution, which turned the centuries-old power structure upside down. In July of that year Mwami Mutara III Rudahigwa, otherwise known as King Charles, died in the Burundian capital. The Belgians said the cause of death was a heart attack, but angry rumors claimed that the king had been assassinated—by militant Hutus or by disgruntled Tutsis, depending on the source of the rumor. Hutu-Tutsi communal violence escalated. At Mutara III's funeral his brother, Kigeri V Ndahindurwa, was proclaimed king by the monarchist Tutsis. But the monarchy was in its death throes. A violent Hutu uprising in November 1959 resulted in the deaths of 10,000 Tutsis, particularly in the north of the country, and forced 200,000 Tutsis—about a third of the Tutsi population—to flee across the borders. The royal family had to be rescued by Belgian paratroopers.

PARMEHUTU won a general election in 1960. The Hutu overthrow of the feudal order was completed when Rwanda was proclaimed a republic on January 28, 1961. In September Rwandans overwhelmingly voted for the abolition of the monarchy in a referendum organized by the United Nations. On July 1,

1962, the Belgian-administered United Nations Territories of Rwanda and Burundi became independent. Grégoire Kayibanda became the first president of the Republic of Rwanda. In Burundi the Tutsi royal family remained constitutional monarchs of their newly independent country.

A second general election in October 1963 resulted in PARMEHUTU winning every seat in the parliament. Across the border in Burundi, Zaire, Uganda, and Tanzania, Tutsi exiles who had been organizing since 1961 launched three unsuccessful invasions of their homeland at the end of 1963. In retaliation, the Hutu government of Rwanda repressed Tutsis, up to 14,000 of whom were killed in the space of about two months.

A decade of ethnic politics followed, during which many Tutsis were systematically excluded from all walks of life and barred from schools and universities under a 10 percent quota system. Further massacres of Tutsis occurred in 1967 and 1973.

In July 1973, President Kayibanda was ousted in a bloodless coup by General Juvénal Habyarimana, a northwesterner. Promising to end the ethnic troubles, Habyarimana dissolved PARMEHUTU.

PERSECUTION OF THE TUTSIS

Unfortunately, Habyarimana's ascent ushered in 20 years of progressively greater marginalization of the Tutsi people. In practice, intermarriage still occurred. Tutsi women commonly married Hutu men, but Hutu families were very wary of allowing their daughters to marry Tutsis. In the changed world of Rwanda, Tutsis were reduced to eking out a living at the margins of agriculture, often by tending their small herds of cattle, and a Hutu woman who married a Tutsi would face a life of hardship and risk. Only a few of the former Tutsi elite remained in the country.

Juvénal Habyarimana. After he deposed President Kayibanda in a bloodless coup in 1973, Habyarimana promised to end Rwanda's ethnic strife. But his two decades in power were marked by increasing marginalization of Tutsis.

In 1975 Habyarimana established a new party, the Mouvement Républicain National pour la Démocratie et le Développement (MRND). Its stated goals were to promote peace, unity, and national development. As a distant popular echo of the unpopular Tutsi reforms of the late 19th century, the new Hutu movement was organized from the "hillside" to the national level. A general election in December 1978 overwhelmingly endorsed a new constitution and confirmed Habyarimana as president. He was reelected in 1983 and again in 1988.

Habyarimana had commanded popular support and high hopes for a more equitable Rwanda when he seized power in 1973. Tutsis were to enjoy "*equilibre*"—a 15 percent share of educational and employment opportunities to reflect their proportion of the population. But the identity card policy was continued, ostensibly to enforce *equilibre*.

As the years wore on, however, the president relied more and more on a hard-line inner circle of Hutu extremists. These advisers were drawn mainly from Habyarimana's home area in the northwest. Habyarimana protected and isolated himself with a presidential guard and co-opted Catholic Church leaders and leaders of the embryonic trade union movement to the MRND's cause. Through new MRND-led cooperatives in the countryside and the establishment of a national network of Hutu militia units, Habyarimana's government was able to tightly monitor events throughout Rwanda.

Dissent became dangerous, and eventually all political activity was banned. A census was suppressed when it revealed the extent of Tutsi-Hutu mixed marriages in Rwanda. Hutu soldiers were forbidden to take Tutsi wives. Government-controlled media pumped out a constant diet of anti-Tutsi propaganda and lies. By 1990 there was just one Tutsi cabinet member, and moderate Hutus, especially those from the south and central regions of the country, were becoming increasingly alienated from their one-party government. Many fled abroad to join the Tutsi-led rebels.

COUNTDOWN TO GENOCIDE

In Tanzania the Rwandan refugees were welcomed but firmly told to stay in their camps along the borders. They could not become Tanzanian citizens.

In Uganda, however, Rwanda's refugees soon became embroiled in the politics of their host nation, which suffered first under the dictatorship of Dr. Milton Obote and then under the infamous Idi Amin. Many Rwandans joined the Ugandan army, and in 1979 they found themselves caught up in Uganda's civil war, which followed Tanzania's invasion to topple Amin.

Rwandan exiles in Uganda eventually formed the Rwandan Patriotic Front (RPF). It was dedicated to overthrowing the

MRND regime in Kigali, the Rwandan capital. The RPF drew its ranks from 1959 exiles, refugees from the 1963 and 1973 massacres, and guerrillas who were fighting with Yoweri Museveni's National Resistance Army (NRA), which in 1986 brought peace to Uganda. Four years later, in October 1990, the battle-hardened RPF invaded Rwanda from Uganda.

The Habyarimana government immediately branded Tutsis still in Rwanda as rebel accomplices. Fighting raged for six months, but with the support of French troops, the Rwandan army succeeded in stopping the RPF offensive. In March 1991 a ceasefire was signed, but it soon broke down and fighting resumed.

In June, under pressure from foreign aid donors, Habyarimana agreed to abandon one-party rule in favor of a multiparty democracy. This greatly agitated hard-line members of the ruling MRND. But to some observers Habyarimana's commitment to a more inclusive government appeared lukewarm. Even while the president was producing proposals for a new multiparty constitution and publicly affirming his support for power sharing, critics of the government were being persecuted and hundreds of Tutsis murdered. At the same time, with French backing, Habyarimana increased the size of Rwanda's armed forces from 3,000 to 30,000. Even more disturbing, the Rwandan army was arming and training Hutu civilian militias known as *Interahamwe* (meaning "those who attack together").

In April 1992 a coalition government was finally formed. The MRND held onto 9 of the 19 ministries, and Habyarimana remained president. Still, many MRND officials feared that their party's days in power were numbered. Some even suggested that competition among various Hutu opposition parties would dilute Hutu power and inevitably help Tutsis take control of Rwanda's government once again.

Such ethnically based arguments may have seemed compelling, but at most they reflected a part of MRND members' true concerns. In Rwanda, as in other impoverished African countries, the party or group in power often controls the use and distribution of the nation's fiscal resources (such as tax revenues and foreign aid money) and holds the key to highly coveted government jobs (in Rwanda during the years leading up to the genocide, there were about 50,000 government posts, at the national and local levels). This control typically translates into a privileged economic and social status for the ruling group. It also provides a means to placate supporters, and thus to remain in power.

For their part, Rwanda's newly formed opposition parties were eager to gain access to a share of revenues and resources, which the MRND resisted. As the parties competed, Hutu-on-Hutu political tensions simmered, occasionally bubbling over into violence.

In July 1992 the Rwandan government and the RPF signed another cease-fire. The following month the warring parties opened talks aimed at finding a political resolution to the conflict.

In February 1993, however, the RPF launched a new offensive. Only French intervention prevented the rebels from taking Kigali. "Ethnic problems will end when the war ends," declared an outwardly optimistic President Habyarimana in March.

In August the president and the RPF signed a peace agreement in the Tanzanian city of Arusha. Under the terms of the agreement, called the Arusha Accords, refugees would be permitted to return to Rwanda, and the Rwandan army and the RPF would merge. In addition, a coalition government would be established. It would be led by a Hutu prime minister, but 5 of the 21 cabinet posts would be reserved for Tutsis.

To prevent a resumption of the civil war and aid in the implementation of the Arusha Accords, a 2,500-man United Nations peacekeeping force—the United Nations Assistance Mission for Rwanda, or UNAMIR—was dispatched to Kigali. After all the bloodshed, peace seemed to be within reach.

But Hutu extremists weren't committed to the sharing of power or resources. The training of Hutu militias accelerated, and a constant stream of anti-Tutsi propaganda was broadcast over the Hutu-controlled Radio-Télévision Libre des Mille Collines (Free Radio and Television of a Thousand Hills) and disseminated in the print media. International human rights groups and the commander of UNAMIR warned that Rwanda was on the verge of a cataclysm of ethnic violence.

100 DAYS OF TERROR

On April 6, 1994, a plane carrying President Habyarimana and President Cyprien Ntaryamira of Burundi was shot down by a missile as it approached Kigali Airport. Both heads of state were killed.

It remains unclear who was responsible for the assassinations, though many experts suspect Hutu extremists angered at Habyarimana's acceptance of the Arusha Accords. In any case, the downing of the presidential plane seems to have initiated a

These Rwandan Patriotic Front rebels were photographed near Ngarama in February 1993, shortly after a renewed RPF offensive doomed a cease-fire that had been in effect since the previous July.

Hutu Interahamwe militiamen, Gitarama, Rwanda, June 1994. Among the militias, the machete was a favorite tool for slaughter.

well-orchestrated plan. Within half an hour—before news of Habyarimana's death had been made public—soldiers and Interahamwe militiamen were searching for and murdering journalists, human rights advocates, and prominent Hutu moderates. Rwanda's prime minister, Agathe Uwilingiyimana, was among the early Hutu victims. Rwandan soldiers also killed 10 Belgian peacekeepers assigned to protect Uwilingiyimana, which factored into the UN's decision to reduce the size of the UNAMIR contingent from 2,500 to 250. Throughout the unfolding crisis, UNAMIR soldiers lacked the mandate to use force to protect victims of the murderous violence.

The slaughter of Tutsis also began almost immediately after the downing of President Habyarimana's plane. Interahamwe set up blockades in the streets, checked identity cards, and murdered any Tutsis they found. Roving gangs of Hutus burst into homes, beating and hacking to death their Tutsi neighbors with whatever weapons they had at their disposal—clubs, iron bars, machetes, hammers. Soldiers and militiamen overran churches and schools where terrified Tutsis had sought refuge, killing their victims with guns, grenades, and machetes.

Throughout, the killers were urged on by the broadcasts of the Kigali-based Radio-Télévision Libre des Mille Collines, which had for months been telling Hutus they'd been "shamed" by Tutsis under colonial rule and offering rallying cries like "Be Proud of Your Hutu Blood!" The broadcasts had also demonized Tutsis as "cockroaches" (*inyenzi*) that needed "exterminating." After April 6, the commands were direct. "All those who are listening rise so that we can fight for Rwanda!" the radio station exhorted Hutus. "Fight with the weapons you have at your disposal! Those who have arrows—fight with arrows! Those who have spears—fight with spears! We must not fail!"

While the killing may have been led by soldiers and members of the state-sponsored Interahamwe militias, the personal involvement of ordinary Rwandans from all walks of life is perhaps the most disturbing aspect of the genocide. Teachers killed their Tutsi students. Doctors killed their Tutsi patients. Husbands killed their Tutsi wives. Even priests aided the killers and in some cases took part in the slaughter. Hutus who refused to kill Tutsis were themselves killed.

AFTERMATH

In the days immediately following April 6, the enormity of the situation in Rwanda became apparent. Nevertheless, the international community failed to act to end the genocide.

Victims of the Rwandan genocide.

From northern Rwanda, RPF troops launched a renewed offensive, advancing steadily. Hundreds of thousands of ordinary Hutus, fearing reprisals, fled Rwanda ahead of the RPF forces. Hiding in the midst of these refugees were many of the extremists who had masterminded and directed the genocide. By July 4 the RPF had swept into Kigali. Two weeks later, on the 18th, the last extremist Hutu forces were routed from the northwestern part of the country. Paul Kagame, the RPF leader, declared Rwanda's civil war over. A new, multiparty coalition government was formed. It quickly signaled its intention to implement the Arusha Accords and abandon Rwanda's ethnic classification system.

How the Rwandan genocide could occur is a question that defies simple answers. Much of the initial media coverage explained the killing as a spontaneous eruption of pent-up, ancient tribal feuding. That explanation clearly does not withstand scrutiny: the genocide was not spontaneous but meticulously planned and fueled by a relentless propaganda campaign; besides, the ethnic categories Tutsi and Hutu were, until relatively recent times, fluid. Nor was the genocide an inevitable consequence of the divide-and-rule policies of colonial administrators, though those policies surely contributed. Whatever roots it may have had in the past, the Rwandan genocide was also the result of a very modern power struggle, a struggle for control of severely limited resources in a society where all democratic restraints had been removed.

For the Hutu elite, which had ruled Rwanda since the overthrow of the Tutsi monarchy—and particularly for those who had benefited during the long and dictatorial regime of Juvénal Habyarimana—the kind of compromises required by the Arusha Accords would have diminished their position considerably. If Tutsis were to be included in the government, some Hutus would inevitably have to give up their government

The genocide, and the RPF offensive that finally ended it, created hundreds of thousands of refugees.

posts—and their control of government revenues. If the RPF were to be merged with the Rwandan armed forces, not only would a percentage of the Hutu officer corps be replaced by Tutsis, but thousands of Hutu soldiers would also be dismissed to make room for RPF replacements. Beyond the inconveniences imposed by the Arusha Accords, however, the Hutu elite faced an inescapable reality: if ordinary Hutus concluded that their leaders weren't providing for them anymore, then the status quo could not be maintained. The Hutu elite's days in power would be numbered. Blaming Tutsis for all of Rwanda's problems served to deflect attention away from the failings of extremist Hutu rule.

That Hutus at the lower rungs of Rwandan society would be moved by anti-Tutsi propaganda is perhaps not too surprising. The collapse of coffee prices had devastated the economy of an already impoverished country. Hunger was spreading. The majority of Rwandans relied on subsistence agriculture for their

Too little, too late: British peacekeepers arrive in Kigali Airport, August 1994. According to Romeo Dallaire, the commander of the United Nations Assistance Mission for Rwanda, hundreds of thousands of lives could had been saved had the international community quickly reinforced his 2,500-man contingent after the genocide began.

livelihood, and the supply of farmland was diminishing as the country's population expanded rapidly. Relentless propaganda portrayed Tutsis as aliens, as invaders on land that rightly belonged to Hutus. It is no accident that the genocide leaders urged Hutus to kill their Tutsi neighbors and "eat their cows"—or that after the Tutsis were dead, their houses and other possessions were looted.

The RPF-led government that replaced the Hutu extremists in 1994 took pains to remove the corrosive effects of ethnicity from Rwandan politics. Members of all ethnic groups were included in the new government. The identity card system was abandoned. There was no organized retaliation against Hutus.

However, in late 1994 Rwandan authorities began arresting more than 120,000 people who had participated in the genocide. This was more than the justice system could handle. Eventually, a system of Gacaca courts was established, where villagers and judges woulc convene to try those accused of local genocide crimes. High-level leaders from the government, military, media, and church were to be tried by the International Criminal Tribunal for Rwanda (ICTR), which was established by the United Nations in Arusha, Tanzania. As of 2013, this body was still conducting trials.

Unfortunately, the Hutu-Tutsi conflict eventually extended beyond Rwanda's borders. In 1996, the Rwandan government sent troops into Zaire (now the Democratic Republic of the Congo, or DRC) to attack Hutu refugee camps that they believed had become sites of military organizing. The Rwandan government claimed that many of the refugees were being held hostage by these forces. It wanted the refugee population to return to Rwanda to reintegrate into society and, when necessary, to face justice. It also wanted to remove the potential threat of an invasion by Hutu extremists.

In 1997, Rwandan forces joined with Zairean rebels to depose President Mobutu Sese Seko, who was supporting the Hutu extremists. When Sese Seko stepped down in 1998, Laurent Kabila became president. However, Kabila refused to expel Hutu extremist militias from the country, so Rwanda again joined with opposition forces. The resulting conflict, known as the Second Congo War, was the deadliest war in African history, with eight nations and numerous armed factions involved. More than 5.4 million people were killed, and millions more became refugees. Although a peace agreement was supposed to end the fighting in 2003, areas of conflict still remain.

6 CONCLUSION

In the 19th century, "tribalism" was the lens through which European explorers, colonialists, and anthropologists tended to view African political and social organization and—because they knew almost nothing about the subject—African history. Today, the inadequacy of that approach is universally acknowledged. Africa is simply too large, too complex, and too diverse to reduce the trajectory of the continent to a simple narrative of ethnic factors.

Yet in the case of conflicts in individual African countries, journalists and other outside observers sometimes attribute the problems to "fundamental" differences between ethnic groups, and they often note that the groups' grievances against one another are many centuries old. Often such explanations are oversimplified. They may, for example, gloss over underlying economic causes of a conflict; they may overlook the fact that ethnic categories can be quite fluid rather than set in stone.

But ethnicity cannot be dismissed entirely as a factor in many African conflicts. This is true even when history has been distorted and manipulated, and ethnic differences have been magnified, for political ends. Before the Rwanda genocide, for example, it may have been impossible to distinguish a Hutu from a Tutsi on the basis of racial origin, physical appearance, or language. Hutus and Tutsis had occupied the same territory and had intermarried for centuries. Yet the very fact that over the course of a few decades Hutu extremists were able to marginalize Tutsis as "invaders" and "cockroaches"—and that ordinary Hutus from all walks of life were willing to murder them indiscriminately—testifies to the powerful pull of ethnicity-based appeals.

It should be emphasized that Africa isn't the only place where unscrupulous leaders have, in recent decades, exploited communal grievances with tragic results. In Yugoslavia, for example, appeals to Serbian nationalism touched off a brutal series of civil wars during the 1990s, claiming the lives of hundreds of thousands and causing the country to fracture along ethnic lines.

SOLUTIONS

In Africa and the rest of the world, large-scale ethnically based conflicts frequently occur where economic resources are in short supply, where democratic institutions are weak, and where winner-take-all politics prevail. Under such circumstances, appeals to ethnic solidarity may resonate with people struggling for a decent standard of living, angry that they are not getting their fair share of government spending, and fearful of being politically dominated by members of another group.

More responsible and competent governance could go a long way toward defusing ethnic tensions in Africa. Economic development benefiting all segments of society, and political institutions giving all citizens a voice in their government, would serve to unite rather than divide Africa's many ethnic groups.

Glossary

CALIPHATE—the territory ruled by an Islamic leader who is regarded as a successor to the prophet Muhammad.

CLAN—a group of people related by blood or marriage who can usually trace their origins to a common ancestor.

COMMUNAL—relating to or based on ethnic, racial, or cultural groups.

COUP—a sudden and decisive change of government, usually by a small group using force or the threat of force; also called a coup d'etat.

CULTURE—the set of shared values, beliefs, customs, and traits, including language, that form the basis of a group's self-identity and distinguish one people from another.

CUSTOM—a long-established belief or way of behaving; a tradition.

DIALECT—a regional variety of a language.

GENOCIDE—the deliberate and systematic destruction of a racial or cultural group.

INDIGENOUS—born in or belonging naturally to a region or country.

JIHAD—a war waged by Muslims who claim to be acting in defense of their faith.

NATIONALISM—promotion of the interests or culture of one's own ethnic group or nation above the interests or culture of other groups; national consciousness, especially when accompanied by the desire for an independent state.

NOMADIC—relating to or characteristic of a lifestyle in which people have no fixed residence but instead move from place to place (often seasonally).

REFUGEES—people who have fled their home country to find safety in another.

REVENUE—government income from taxation, investments, rent, and export earnings.

SAVANNA—tropical and subtropical grasslands with scattered trees.

SULTAN—a king or sovereign of a Muslim state.

Further Reading

Binns, Tony, Alan Dixon, and Etienne Nel. *Africa: Diversity and Development*. New York: Routledge, 2012.

Burr, J. Millard, and Robert O. Collins. *Africa's Thirty Years' War: Chad, Libya, and the Sudan, 1963–1993*. Boulder, Colo.: Westview Press, 1999.

Crisafulli, Patricia, and Andrea Redmond. *Rwanda, Inc.: How a Devastated Nation Became an Economic Model for the Developing World.* New York: Palgrave Macmillan, 2012.

Collier, Paul et al. *Breaking the Conflict Trap: Civil War and Development Policy.* Washington, D.C.: World Bank/Oxford University Press, 2003.

Dowden, Richard. *Africa: Altered States, Ordinary Miracles*. New York: Public Affairs, 2010.

De Waal, Alex. *Famine that Kills: Darfur, Sudan* (Oxford Studies in African Affairs). Rev. ed. New York: Oxford University Press, USA, 2005.

De Waal, Alex, and Julie Flint. *Darfur: A Short History of a Long War* (African Arguments). London: Zed Books, 2006.

Edelstein, Jillian. *Truth & Lies: Stories from the Truth and Reconciliation Commission in South Africa*. New York: The New Press, 2002.

Ehret, Christopher. *The Civilizations of Africa: A History to 1800.* Oxford: James Currey Publishers, 2004.

Gourevitch, Philip. *We Wish to Inform You That Tomorrow We Will Be Killed with Our Families.* New York: Farrar, Straus and Giroux, 1998.

Hardin, Victoria A. *AIDS at 30: A History*. Washington, D.C.: Potomac Books, 2012.

Hatzfeld, Jean. *Into the Quick of Life: The Rwandan Genocide—The Survivors Speak*. London: Serpent's Tail, 2005.

Horowitz, Donald L. *The Deadly Ethnic Riot*. Berkeley and Los Angeles: University of California Press, 2003.

Human Rights Watch. *They Do Not Own This Place: Government Discrimination Against "Non-Indigenes" in Nigeria*. Lagos and New York: Human Rights Watch, 2006.

Imobighe A. Thomas, ed. *Civil Society and Ethnic Conflict Management in Nigeria*. Ibadan, Nigeria: Spectrum Books, 2003.

Johnson, Douglas H. *The Root Causes of Sudan's Civil Wars* (African Issues). Bloomington: Indiana University Press, 2003.

Keane, Fergal. *A Season of Blood*. New York: Penguin Books USA, 1995.

Mbanaso, Michael U. and Chima J. Korieh, eds. *Minorities and the State in Africa*. Amherst, NY: Cambria Press, 2010.

Meredith, Martin. *The Fate of Africa: A History of the Continent Since Independence*. New York: Public Affairs, 2011.

Miguel, Edward. *Africa's Turn?* Cambridge, Mass.: MIT Press, 2009.

Moseley, William. *Taking Sides: Clashing Views on African Issues*. New York: McGraw Hill, 2011.

Natsios, Andrew S. *Sudan, South Sudan, and Darfur: What Everyone Needs to Know*. New York: Oxford University Press, 2012.

Peel, Michael. *A Swamp Full of Dollars: Pipelines and Paramilitaries at Nigeria's Oil Frontier*. Chicago: Chicago Review Press, 2010.

Radelet, Steven. *Emerging Africa: How 17 Countries are Leading the Way*. Washington, D.C.: Center for Global Development, 2010.

Rotberg, Robert I. *Transformative Political Leadership: Making a Difference in the Developing World*. Chicago: University of Chicago Press, 2012.

Shillington, Kevin. *History of Africa*. New York: Palgrave Macmillan, 2012.

Suberu, RT. *Ethnic Minority, Conflict, and Governance in Nigeria*. Ibadan: Spectrum Books, 1996.

Williams, Paul D. *War and Conflict in Africa*. Malden, Mass.: Polity Press, 2011.

Internet Resources

HTTPS://WWW.CIA.GOV/LIBRARY/PUBLICATIONS/THE-WORLD-FACTBOOK

The CIA World Factbook provides a wealth of background and statistical information, including percentages of ethnic groups, for all the world's countries.

HTTP://WWW.UNESCO.ORG/MOST/P95.HTM

Ethno-Net Africa, "a network for comparative studies, monitoring and evaluation of ethnic conflicts and social transformation in Africa," provides a country-by-country list of ethnic conflicts on the continent.

HTTP://WWW.UNESCO.ORG/NEW/EN/CULTURE/THEMES/ENDANGERED-LANGUAGES/

The United Nations Educational, Scientific and Cultural Organization (UNESCO) provides information about endangered African languages, as well as an interactive map, at this site.

HTTP://WWW.AEGISTRUST.ORG

Website of Aegis Trust, a nongovernmental organization that focuses on genocide prevention and education and is active in Darfur and Rwanda.

HTTP://WWW.IPACC.ORG.ZA

The website of the Indigenous Peoples of Africa Coordinating Committee offers information about marginalized nomadic and aboriginal peoples of Africa.

HTTP://WWW.NIGERIA.GOV.NG

News and information about Nigeria, Africa's most populous country.

HTTP://WWW.ICTR.ORG

The International Criminal Tribunal for Rwanda is trying cases from that country's 1994 genocide.

HTTP://HRW.ORG/ENGLISH/DOCS/2006/04/24/NIGERI13260.HTM

This summary of a Human Rights Watch report on indigeneity policies in Nigeria includes a link to the full report.

Index

Numbers in ***bold italic*** refer to captions.

Picture Credits

Page

2: Corbis Images
9: © OTTN Publishing
12: PhotoSphere
14: Vilem Bischof/AFP/Getty Images
15: Corbis Images
18: Hornig/DPA/Landov
21: © OTTN Publishing
23: Joy Tessman/National Geographic/Getty Images
24: Corbis Images
25: Corbis Images
27: A. Fleuret/US AID
31: © OTTN Publishing
33: Krzystzof Grzymski/Saudi Aramco World/PADIA
37: Randy Olson/National Geographic/Getty Images
39: Jiro Ose/Reuters/Landov
40: Library of Congress
42: Bert Hardy/Picture Post/Getty Images
47: Manoocher Deghati/AFP/Getty Images
48: Mike Nelson/AFP/Getty Images
49: Thomas Mukoya/Reuters/Landov
51: Scott Nelson/Getty Images
53: Scott Nelson/Getty Images
58: Dave Clark/AFP/Getty Images
60: © OTTN Publishing
61: Courtesy José Cruz/Agência Brasil
62: Jacob Silberberg/Getty Images
63: George Esiri/Reuters/Landov
65: Malcolm Linton/Liaison/Getty Images
69: Juda Ngwenya/Reuters/Landov
71: UN Photo
72: Hulton Archive/Getty Images
74: Francois Rojon/AFP/Getty Images
76: UN Photo
77: UN Photo
79: Antony Njuguna/Reuters/Landov
81: © OTTN Publishing
83: Scott Peterson/Liaison/Getty Images
86: Henry Guttmann/Hulton Archive/Getty Images
87: Howard Davies/Corbis
89: Bettmann/Corbis
92: Templeton/U.S. Department of Defense
96: Alexander Joe/AFP/Getty Images
97: Alexander Joe/AFP/Getty Images
99: Msgt. Rose Reynolds/U.S. Department of Defense
101: Tech. Sgt. Lemuel Cassilas/U.S. Department of Defense
102: Tsgt. Marvin Krause/U.S. Department of Defense

Contributors

Professor Robert I. Rotberg currently holds the Fulbright Research Chair in Political Development at the Balsillie School of International Affairs in Waterloo, Canada. Prior to this, from 1999 to 2010 he served as director of the Program on Intrastate Conflict and Conflict Resolution at the Kennedy School, Harvard University. He is the author of a number of books and articles on Africa, including *Transformative Political Leadership: Making a Difference in the Developing World* (2012) and *"Worst of the Worst": Dealing with Repressive and Rogue Nations* (2007). Professor Rotberg is president emeritus of the World Peace Foundation.

Dr. Victor Ojakorotu is head of the Department of Politics and International Relations at North-West University in Mafikeng, South Africa. He earned his Ph.D. from the University of the Witwatersrand, Johannesburg, in 2007, and has published numerous articles on African politics and environmental issues. North-West University is one of the largest institutions of higher education in South Africa, with 64,000 students enrolled at three campuses.

Elizabeth Obadina is a writer, journalist, and teacher who began working on development projects in Nigeria in the early 1970s. For 20 years she lived primarily in Lagos and London, working for the British Broadcasting Corporation (BBC), *The Times* (London), *New Internationalist*, UNICEF, and other UN organizations and international radio broadcasters as a freelance writer and news reporter about Africa. Since 1995 she has lived in Shropshire, England, with her husband and three grown-up children, working as a teacher and writer of adult education booklets, which support documentaries produced by Independent Television (ITV), Britain's leading commercial broadcaster.